Remarkable Women of New England

Daughters, Wives, Sisters, and Mothers

The War Years 1754 to 1787

Carole Owens

Globe Pequot

Guilford, Connecticut

For Ari and Ella
The next generation
For Mary and Todd
The best of this generation

Globe Pequot

An imprint of Rowman & Littlefield

Distributed by NATIONAL BOOK NETWORK

Copyright © 2016 by Carole Owens

British Library Cataloguing in Publication Information Available

Library of Congress Cataloging-in-Publication Data
Owens, Carole, author.
  Remarkable women of New England : daughters, wives, sisters, and mothers : the war years 1754 to 1787 / Carole Owens. — First edition.
     pages cm
  Includes bibliographical references and index.
  ISBN 978-1-4930-1668-6 (pbk. : alk. paper) — ISBN 978-1-4930-1845-1 (e-book) 1.
Women—New England—History—18th century. 2. Women—New England—Social conditions—18th century. I. Title.
  HQ1438.N35O93 2015
  305.4097409'033—dc23

2015036277

∞™ The paper used in this publication meets the minimum requirements of American National Standard for Information Sciences—Permanence of Paper for Printed Library Materials, ANSI/NISO Z39.48-1992.

Contents

Esther Edwards Burr—the wife of Aaron Burr Sr. and
mother of Aaron Burr Jr. Her husband founded Princeton
University, and her son was the second vice president of
the United States, favorite son and then tried for treason.
Elizabeth was an avid journal keeper.

Lavinia Deane Fisk—widowed during the Revolutionary
War, her second marriage triggered a firestorm. It led to
a revolutionary war in the Congregational Church. The
written record of the subsequent ecclesiastic and civil
court actions tell her story.

The Widow Bingham—also widowed during the war but
chose a very different path. Far from seeking to remarry,
she fought to live as a man, becoming the first woman to
have a tavern license, build a business substantial enough
to send her son to college, and serve on formerly all-male
civic committees, such as the highway commission.

Mary Gray Bidwell—a quiet country woman who, through
her relations, witnessed history and aided her husband as a
war was fought and a new nation formed.

List of Illustrations

Acknowledgments

Recounting history is like playing with children's blocks: one account rests on another. I am deeply indebted to a number of authors who preceded me and made a contribution to our collective understanding of the women of eighteenth-century America. Their books are listed in the bibliography.

I sincerely thank local historian Lion Miles, exceptional family historian Richard Bidwell Wilcox, and Yale University student Jonah Bader for their careful and thorough research. Thank you to history teacher Eleanor Clary and MCLA professor Mary Levitt for your time reading and generosity in commenting on the text. Thank you to Mary Hart, the only person I ever met who liked indexing. Thank you to my "assistant" Chris Baumann, with special appreciation for each and every one of his hats.

As always the contribution of the Local History Room of the Berkshire Athenaeum under the leadership of Kathleen Reilly is unmatched; thank you Ann Marie Harris, Don Warfield, Rick Leab, Rita Martin, and Maureen Marrone.

I am also grateful to Yale University for use of its collections and to Boston University for the excellent "Dublin Series." In addition I thank the towns and churches of Lenox, Pittsfield, Stockbridge, and Great Barrington, Massachusetts, for use of their records, and Massachusetts Archives for use of the early court records of Hampshire and Berkshire Counties. Massachusetts figures prominently in this retelling because in the Commonwealth records are carefully preserved and generously made available.

To William D. Miles and other private collectors who have saved and curate their families' documents and artifacts, and have shared them with me, in heartfelt gratitude, thank you.

To all those who know the value of history, who preserve and protect the record, and share it; those who protect and restore the artifacts big and small from a house to a snuff box, thank you.

Author's Note

Quotations may be altered in the following manner: when necessary for clarity, spelling, and capitalization are corrected.

Some scholars choose to spell the word as it appeared—for example, "setld"—and then in brackets correct it for the modern reader like this "setld [settled]." I respect the effort but find it hopelessly muddles the text. Equally many historians faithfully transcribe the unique capitalization pattern of the eighteenth century, such as:

> *The Schuyler family which Rendered so much good Service to New England is the same Family that includes this Gentleman and lived in this Township.*

One might guess the pattern of capitalization was done for emphasis or alternately to indicate respect. What it does not do is enhance the meaning; therefore the capitalization has been corrected and follows modern rules.

In the footnotes I use the abbreviation SML, which stands for Sterling Memorial Library. The unabbreviated reference is "Yale University Manuscripts and Archives Division Sterling Memorial Library."

In this book, I deal exclusively with village life. We are content to live among strangers; they were not. Perhaps with a population of over 300 million, we have no choice. The "Colonies" had a population of approximately 1.5 million. Boston was considered a roiling population center with 17,000. Even as the nineteenth century approached, America was an intimate world. It was horse-drawn, candle-lit, and sylvan. The population of the entire country grew to just 5 million with only 6 percent living in cities. The rest lived in the countryside. For that reason this book deals with life in New England villages and not city life.

In order to include all of the elements that would have been familiar to an eighteenth-century woman, the village in this book is a composite. It relies heavily upon Stockbridge, Massachusetts, a New England village founded in 1739 that thrived throughout the period. However, the posting of the elopement did not occur in Stockbridge but in Bennington, Vermont. The "warning out" mentioned took place in Pittsfield, Massachusetts. The regulation house was built in Williamstown. They are included, as are other elements, because they were a common part, and offer the reader a fuller understanding, of eighteenth-century New England village life.

The homestead described is also a composite. To present the context in which eighteenth-century women lived, all the elements had to be included whether they existed in a single establishment or not. The parts of an eighteenth-century woman's homestead were the house, dooryard, gardens, outbuildings, a water source, and water storage. The descriptions are taken from the wills of John Deane of Stockbridge, his father-in-law Daniel Higby of Sheffield, and the Reverend Thomas Allen of Pittsfield, as well as period descriptions of fortified houses. Inside the fittings are from a book kept by an eighteenth-century father living in Connecticut. The sum exposes the reader to the eighteenth-century household.

It may be the general rule to create a composite of voices and vignettes from the past, to make a point and illustrate it with multiple examples, moments in different lives once lived. Herein you will meet the same people over and over again. They will act in different contexts and interact with different people. The hope is that in this book, as in life, you will meet them, grow to know them, and through them understand their world.

The records of the Congregational Church relied upon are from the First Congregational Churches of Stockbridge, Sheffield, Pittsfield, and Great Barrington, Massachusetts, and are presented as representative of the eighteenth-century New England Congregational Church. However, while the Congregational Church was dominant in eighteenth-century New England, there were also Quaker meetinghouses, Dutch Reform Churches, a synagogue or two, "the King's Churches" (Episcopalian), Catholic and Baptist Churches, and "heathen" (the unaffiliated).

The title of this book includes the term *New England*. However, during the Revolutionary War the text expands beyond New England. For example, the Schuyler estate was in New York and Emily Geiger rode through South Carolina. Just as the colonies expanded to unite all the colonies in the war against England, so this text expands to include stories of brave women from beyond New England.

In Part I the woman's place is explained. Chapter 1 is an overview of the life of an eighteenth-century woman. The next four chapters define the four corners of her world: home lot, church, village, and social circle. Chapter 6 describes the laws that shaped and limited her experience. Chapter 7 is about women in war. Each chapter includes first exposition, and then that is illustrated by the life experiences of one or more women.

Part II is a brief journey into the post-Revolutionary period and the early nineteenth century when education, work, sexual mores, and laws change. Church doctrine is supplanted by the etiquette book, the Bible is superseded by the novel, and her world expands beyond the hearthside.

The Appendices describe that women in the eighteenth century did not rule the world in which they lived. They were not central figures but peripheral in government, business, religion, and the arts. To understand their experience, one must understand the things that shaped their world, things in which they had no part. Discussions of religion, politics, events, and ideas that did not include women but affected them are found in the appendices.

Part One

The Four Corners of a Woman's World

Chapter 1

Introduction

I Notable

I have a great and longing desire to be very notable.[1]

It is important to give the eighteenth-century definition of the phrase *notable woman*. Today we would define a notable woman as distinguished, prominent, or famous. That definition bears little resemblance to what the term meant in the mid- and late eighteenth century. Then, a notable woman was an industrious, frugal, and fruitful wife.

The woman was the chief production officer in the household. She made finished goods out of what her husband supplied: food out of crops, cloth out of cotton and wool, and clothing out of cloth and animal skins. Of the first importance, she produced babies, creating the labor force for whatever the family enterprise was at the time.

An eighteenth-century American wife was an economic arrow in her husband's quiver—an economic asset. The notion of a woman as companion would come later; the notion of a woman as equal partner would come much later.

For now, in the rough American landscape, in the underpopulated continent, a woman was one who could turn raw materials into the needs of the family, who could do it on a shoestring, and who bore many children. A good woman was a useful wife: desirable only as the bringer of goods and filler of needs, not as an individual. An amiable woman was not affable; an amiable woman was compliant and deferential. An

3

Making soap ALICE MORSE EARLE, *HOME LIFE IN COLONIAL DAYS*, 1898, P. 254

attractive woman was not physically appealing; an attractive woman was an agreeable and obedient woman. A homely woman was not ugly, she was domestic. Domestication was the path to her becoming notable.

The meanings of the words such as *notable*, *attractive*, and *amiable* were different because the world was different. It is important to understand and remember the differences, important that we do not assume they were like us but that we become acquainted with them as they were.

These women, unlike the women of today, rarely outlived their husbands. Their life span was markedly shorter; they were used up, buried, and replaced more than once in a man's life.

In eighteenth-century America it was not unusual for a woman to be identified only by her relationship with a man: Mrs. John Jones, the spinster daughter of Mr. John Jones, or the ward of Mr. Jones. Finding something as elementary as the first name of a woman in a household was difficult. Information about a woman's life and accomplishments was even more difficult to discover.

In New England a greater percentage of men were literate than in old England.[2] Fewer women, but still a respectable 40 to 65 percent, were literate. The definition of *literate* is important. The Congregational Church encouraged all members to be able to read their Bible, and in Massachusetts, towns of over fifty citizens were required by law to have an elementary school where boys, and eventually girls, attended. Academies, secondary school, and universities were for men.

The approved education of a woman related to hearth and home: how to make things, how to heal and repair things, how to do things—not read or write about doing them. All a woman's efforts, whether in work or study, were meant for the benefit of her family, not her own enrichment—for her family members, not for those beyond that circle. *Literate* did not mean *educated*.

In 1645 Governor Edward Hopkins of Connecticut consulted the first governor of Massachusetts, John Winthrop.[3] He was concerned because he feared his wife had lost her wits and was suddenly insane. Winthrop said that the origin of the woman's madness was reading books. "If she had attended her household affairs and such things as belong to women, and not gone out of her way and calling to meddle in such things as are proper to men, whose minds are stronger, [she would have] kept her wits."[4]

So the written record is often without the voices of women. Frequently the experiences of women are extrapolated from references to women made by men. Luckily there were exceptions, literate, educated women who kept journals and wrote letters, articles, tracts, poems, plays, and books. Many books about eighteenth-century women include (over and over again) biographies of these same few women: Abigail Adams, Mercy Otis Warren, Deborah Samson Gannett, Molly Pitcher, Nancy Ward, Rachel and Grace Martin.

The list of women illustrates the problem. Repeatedly, authors selected the same women to write about because those were the few women about whom they knew enough, could unearth enough information about to write a book. Three of the women listed above—Sampson and the Martin sisters—distinguished themselves by dressing as men and actually fighting in the Revolutionary War. Mercy Otis Warren was a writer and propagandist. Abigail Adams was First Lady of the United States. Nanyehi, Nancy Ward, was a Cherokee in the Wolf Tribe. The name Nanyehi means "Beloved Woman." The title meant she had power within the tribe, and it was she who negotiated peace between the Cherokee and the Europeans. Molly Pitcher did not exist.

These women were written about simply because there was a record of their lives.

One hundred years later, attitudes had not changed. Ever so slowly girls were accepted into elementary schools. And yet the education of women in the New Republic was thought necessary not for her enrichment but to increase her ability to raise the next generation of male citizens. The women selected for inclusion in this book were all literate. They wrote letters and kept journals considered worth preserving. Therefore it should be remembered that the women mentioned in this book, though hardly household names, were more than exceptions, they were exceptional.

A final word: A "famous woman" was an oxymoron, an impossibility or at least an improbability. An infamous woman, perhaps, but the four corners of an eighteenth-century woman's world precluded any real accomplishment away from hearth and home. The outside world was the province of men.

II   Remarkable

Then in what way were these women remarkable? When Anna Bingham applied for a taverner's license her intent was not to blaze a trail. She did not look over her shoulder to see if other women were following in her footsteps. Anna did not want to establish a beachhead, go where women had been forbidden to go. The Widow Bingham just wanted to feed her son and maintain the roof over her head.

When Lavinia Deane married John Fisk she had no intention of reforming the Congregational Church. She may or may not have been aware that a revival in the Church was being adhered to and challenged in equal measure. She was certainly unaware that she would become the perfect poster child for the power struggle. The Widow Deane just wanted a husband and father for her children. She simply wished to marry the man she loved.

When a goodwife[5] from Vermont fought her husband for possession of the cow, she was not challenging a thousand years of *feme covert*. She did not mean to tear down a pillar of the law. She wanted control of the cow. The cow was a profit center and her husband was a drunk. In a world built on barter, dairy products were currency often traded for other necessities. For the goody, that cow represented economic self-preservation. If she lost control of it, and her husband drank the profits, she and her children could starve, simple as that.

These women did not set out to be remarkable or to change their world. Their motivations were practical. Looking back, we commend their courage and understand how their actions altered institutions and challenged ideas, but they were blissfully unaware and probably pointedly uninterested.

III The Four Corners of Her World

In the well-ordered family, the wife will be "looking upon a husband as her guide . . . recognizing that they are but one mind in two bodies." [6]

It was God's will, and the will of her man, that a woman's life was limited, bound by physical, legal, and social barriers.

Before we meet the women, we might understand their physical world—the four corners beyond which they were discouraged from venturing at all and forbidden from going alone.

The four corners of an eighteenth-century woman's world were the home and garden, the church, the village, and the woman's social circle. A woman could excel in any of these locations, but she had no role and no place outside of them. She was excluded from the village governing bodies. She did not vote or hold office. She might have been excluded from the shops and from the street itself, but that was impractical. Her lowered place in a social hierarchy was unquestioned. By God and man her place was limited; in religion and in law the limitation was justified.

IV Revolution

When this book begins, the definition of a notable woman is clear: there was a hierarchy. God was supreme and reigned over all. Men were subjects of the king, and women were subjects of men. As the text continues, there are rents in the fabric letting in light, and thus illuminated, one sees that things—even if small things—change.

The American Revolution was a bold and heroic event "filled with sound and fury," bloody and long winded. The revolution in women's lives took place at the hearthside—quiet as the hissing flames, delicate as her tea cups, well mannered as Abigail Adams's letters, and about issues as intimate as a kiss goodnight. During the revolution everything was questioned; is it so strange that she also questioned? In its own way, yes, it was remarkable.

And in the end, there is just this: they were people. Before you turn these pages, place a foot in another era, dip a tentative toe in the eighteenth century, know that it was an intimate world; they all knew one another, rubbed up against each other causing friction or warmth, affected one another's lives in ways significant and trivial. Their interactions reveal the peculiarities of an earlier century at the same time that they reveal their common humanity. What they do and say is specific to another time and generally human. Struggle to understand them in context; easily recognize them individually.

Chapter 2

The Homestead

Come tell me how you live.[1]

*Notwithstanding they have so large a family to regulate. The whole is
done with less combustion and noise than many families.*[2]

Isaac Bangs was a young soldier in the Revolutionary War. He was introduced to the Schuyler household, and in his journal, he meant to heap praise upon the lady of the house. To do so, he credited Mrs. Schuyler with regulating her domestic affairs: "She as doth her husband takes pleasure in regulating the affairs of her family, which by her diligence & care is kept in the neatest order & the greatest harmony & decorum may be observed in every department of the whole."[3]

That which was wild and untamed was dangerous and potentially evil. That included the woods surrounding a settlement and the emotions and sexual urges of humankind. The settlement was the regulator of the countryside. Marriage was the regulator of passion. The church was the regulator of the people. The husband and father was the regulator of his household. The plowed field was closer to God than the wilderness, and God was vengeful. When God was redefined as a god of love, the wilds were his habitat. That, however, was in the coming century, for now the goal at home was regulation without "combustion or noise."

The wife was the helpmate of the husband. If she regulated what was under her hand, she was a notable wife.

Within the house the woman's domain included the kitchen, cellars, pantries, and any work rooms such as sewing or spinning rooms.

Note that the nursery was not included. The children, like the many other things she labored to produce, were given to her husband. If she was capable, it was her part to teach them basic literacy—to write their names and read their Bible. After that the boys were turned over to the husband to prepare them for life. The girls remained with the mother to learn their place.

The hierarchy placed her husband first and placed her above the children, but not for long. With the passage of time her sons would exceed her in importance, and grown daughters were her equal or perhaps, depending upon whom they married, her social superior.

In the yard, the brew house, milk house, wash house, and buttery were in her purview. The gardens, animal yards, pig pen, milk yard, hen house, and orchard all fell under her watchful eye. Her domain did not extend across the yard to the fields of corn or wheat, and did not include fishing waters or the mills. While a mill, fields, and waterways may have been part of a homestead, they belonged to the world of men.

In 1749 the General Court in Boston, the overseers of Massachusetts colony appointed by King George, laid out the boundaries of West Hoosac. The following year, the General Court established sixty-three twelve-acre lots that could be claimed by individuals. There was no cost to the claimant, however, to gain title, each had to promise to clear five of the twelve acres for cultivation and build a house in accordance with the regulations set down by the court—in short, build a "regulation house."

In earlier villages established by the court, it had learned its lesson. For example, in Sheffield, the first village established in what is now Berkshire County, land-grant recipients were required to build a road running north out of the village. In their own way, the villagers complied. They cleared a track that was a cart-width (the width of cart wheels), failed to uproot tree stumps or rock outcroppings or smooth the surface, and ended by blazing the trail (marking the trees that ran on either side) to assure that everyone knew that the narrow bumpy way through the woods was a road—of sorts. The villagers may have been satisfied with their compliance but the General Court was not.

Lesson learned. The General Court wrote out the requirements for the houses to be built in West Hoosac. Each house was to be fifteen by eighteen

Colonial kitchen, the heart of the home
ALICE MORSE EARLE, *HOME LIFE IN COLONIAL DAYS*, 1898, P. 164

feet. They could not be finished with rough-hewn planks or logs. The houses were framed out with white oak and the frame was covered with clapboard and shakes. There was no glass for windows, but the windows had wood shutters. If closed against the cold or wet, the shutters blocked the light.

By our standards, the regulation house was small, modest, and barely adequate. However, it took 700 clapboards and 1,000 shakes to cover each house. All were split and shaped by hand. It was a major undertaking and settlers were proud of the result.

At the heart of a regulation house was a stone fireplace—the sole giver of food, warmth, and light. Against the wall, rungs were permanently affixed. At night the occupants climbed the rungs to hammocks slung between rafters—their "beds." The floor was dirt; niceties like floor planks and coverings were impossible luxuries. At the center was a table for all work—sufficient for eating, reading, sewing, calculating, and tinkering. Refrigeration was a hole in the floor.

In the winter of 1752, settlers built the first seven regulation houses in West Hoosac. The would-be landowners traveled far through woodland

Regulation house WILLIAMSTOWN HISTORICAL SOCIETY

and wild country. They labored in the cold, huddled against the wind, framing, studding, and mortising without power, running water, or light after sundown. When completed, the interiors where hardly hospitable, but it was home, and the treasured land was theirs.

The population of West Hoosac grew to twenty-nine people living in fifteen regulation houses. When children were born or relatives were taken in, and the family became larger, the house was enlarged by the simple expedient of adding another fifteen by eighteen box. This addition was built on the other side of the fireplace making the chimney central, heating and lighting both rooms. Traveling through the new village of West Hoosac on horseback, in a wagon, or on "shank's mare" (on foot), anyone could tell at a glance the size of the family by counting the number of fifteen by eighteen additions.

Those were the simple, practical beginnings of a village that is called Williamstown, Massachusetts, today.

Not all Colonials lived in such simplistic dwellings. Along the Connecticut River, the Connecticut "river gods" used their substantial wealth to build homes of surpassing beauty and appreciable size.

Between April and July 1776, Isaac Bangs described the Schuyler estate. At the other end of the economic spectrum from the regulation house, it was equivalent to the Connecticut river mansion: "Mr. Schuyler's house is a large, grand, and magnificent building, built partly of stone and the rest of brick; most beautifully situated on an eminence of the river."[4]

We think first of the government if a road has to be built or water provided to a home. They did not; the householder provided all the necessities for his own homestead, whether large or small. So when Bangs describes the road to the house as "straight and level"[5] he is paying a compliment to Mr. Schuyler. The house has "beautiful groves . . . a most delightful prospect from the front. On the back part of the house is a large neat garden built partly for ornament and partly for convenience [edible and medicinal plants]."[6]

The Schuyler family arrived in the New World two generations prior to the Revolution. Bangs writes that they were of modest means "in tolerable circumstances" when they "accidently discovered copper mines." With the mining profits they bought "contiguous land until they were immensely wealthy."

The establishment that Bangs describes is the result of three generations of prosperity. The occupants of the establishment, described as "one of the first estates of the province," consisted of Mr. and Mrs. Schuyler, their daughter, his sister, her mother, and a brother and his wife forced to flee from New York. There were also fifty to sixty blacks.

"Mrs. Schuyler also seeth to the manufacturing of suitable clothing for the servants."[7] These servants lived in a separate large house built for them. The ringing of a bell turned them out for work in the morning. It rang again at 7:00 a.m. for their breakfast, at noon for their dinner, and at 8:00 p.m. to indicate they could leave work for their home.

The estate had a farm, multiple outbuildings including barns, the servants' residence, and a church. The economic circumstances of the family could be read like words on a page by looking at the house and grounds.

Between the simplicity of the regulation house and the opulence of the Schuyler estate were the middle-class establishments. The arrangements in these middle-class households are gleaned from a number of disparate homesteads around New England. In Stockbridge, Massachusetts,

John Deane made a sale in 1762. In Northampton, the Reverend Jonathan Edwards defended his household arrangements. In Hampton, New Hampshire, Samuel Lane set up housekeeping in 1741.

The subscriber John Deane in consideration of thirty pounds to me in hand and truly said the receipt thereof I [John Deane] do hereby acknowledge do hereby bargain, sell, sell over and convey to Elihu Parsons of Stockbridge his heirs and consigns a Indian woman tenant named Jude aged thirty five years and do hereby deliver over as his servant during his natural life and to his heirs and assigns and do hereby covenant and agree with the Elihu that I have good right to bargain and sell the said Indian woman during her natural life in manner as aforesaid and I will warrant her services accordingly against the lawful claims of all previous whomever and I do hereby declare that I do not know of any sickness or malady of the body attending the said Indian woman. Witness my seal this 13th day— Stockbridge April 13, 1762 in the presence of Timothy Edwards, Justice of the Peace.[8]

What was the woman's life like within the Deane household and subsequently that of Elihu Parsons? There is no record, but this can be said: each of Jude's roles was consistent and reinforced the other. As a woman she was considered a submissive, as a slave she was considered subservient, and as an Indian her social position, her wants, needs, and talents were considered inferior to the white man's, for the proper use of the white man.

Among the inventory of his estate in 1758 was a "negro boy named Titus . . . a negro man named Joseph . . . a negro woman named Sue wife to the said Jo[seph]. . . which slaves were lately the proper goods of said Jonathan Edwards."[9]

Perhaps the fifty or so slaves on the Schuyler estate were expected, but the Deane, Parsons, and Edwards households were middle-class establishments in New England. Titus, Joseph, and Sue were the property of a minister, a man considered to be "the great divine" Jonathan Edwards. His will was executed by his son Timothy Edwards and the slaves were sold for twenty-three pounds "in the open market."[10]

Edwards's slave ownership was neither short-lived nor occasional, nor was it done with a guilty conscience. He owned slaves for at least a quarter of a century and defended the practice in a letter as follows:

> *If they continue to cry out against those who keep Negro slaves, let them also fully and thoroughly vindicate themselves and their own practice in partaking of Negro slavery or confess that there is no hurt in partaking in it. Let them own that their objections are not conscientious.*[11]

Samuel Lane married Mary James on Christmas Eve 1741. He had raised a house in Stratham, New Hampshire, the previous spring in anticipation, and shortly after the New Year, he wrote: "To my great joy and satisfaction got comfortably settled in my own home with an agreeable wife."[12]

The house was twenty-six feet by twenty-nine feet with two chimneys, a great room, and a staircase to the chambers (bedrooms) above. In addition, one room on the ground floor was used as Lane's tanning shop. Compared to a regulation house, Lane's home was grand. Compared to the Schuyler estate, it was merely adequate.

Through his tanning business and by serving as a surveyor, Lane had achieved middle-class comfort. Certainly he was satisfied with his economic position as he felt able to acquire a luxury. He wrote: "Having now got something beforehand [saved] I spoke for [ordered] the clock."[13] His pride comes off the page more than 250 years later: owning a clock was a sign of achievement. Its presence in his home testified to his position in the community.

He and Mary had eight children, five daughters. As each daughter married, she was provided with basic household goods. At times these items were purchased; otherwise they were taken from the Lane household stores. Lane's record keeping describes the daughter's bridal portion; each list was simply titled: "An account of the things I give to my daughter [name] toward her portion."[14]

Lane's lists help us understand how eighteenth-century middle-class households were equipped. Each daughter received two bedsteads. Each bedstead was supplied with cords, a bed, a bolster, and two pillows. The superior of the two beds had higher-quality ticking and more feathers of better quality. We know because Lane was very precise. For example, one bed is described as "made up of 9 yards of fabric valued as sixty-five shillings and 3½ yards more priced at fifty-five shillings ... filled with forty-two pounds of choice feathers. Pillows have thirty two pounds of feathers."[15]

Each bed was supplied with "bed curtains."[16] Of equal importance, each daughter received a brass warming pan to warm the sheets before retiring. The curtains and the brass pan created and conserved warmth, spelled comfort, and represented a significant outlay of cash.

The daughters were provided with bed linens—four to six pairs of sheets and six to twelve pillow cases. Made of linen and cotton, sheets were a costly item. In 1762, a pair of sheets cost eighty-five pounds compared to six chairs, which cost twenty-seven pounds. There was a wool quilt and home-spun quilts with wool fill.

A looking glass was provided and a chest with one drawer plus a case of drawers with brass pulls and locks. There were three tables: one larger oval table for the dining room and two smaller ones, perhaps a side table and a kitchen table. There was a "great chair," perhaps meant for the man of the house? A smaller tufted chair might have been meant for the wife. There was a set of six chairs presumably set around the dining table, and a set of red chairs for the kitchen.

They each received a number of tablecloths either "boughten" or "out of the house." All linens were luxury items, one tablecloth costing ten pounds. All the items, part of the daughter's marriage portion, could be store bought ("readymade"), but, more reflective of woman's work in the eighteenth century, all could be "home spun."

On the practical side, the daughters were given two sheep, foot wheels, and woolen wheels with spindles. The items that were home spun were made by a woman knowing how to raise and tend a sheep shear, card and spin, cut and sew. From barn yard to bed, the notable wife could produce the necessary.

Finally Mr. Lane's daughters each received a clock. Lane intended for all to know that the symbol of his achievements also stood testimony in the five homes of his five married daughters. Samuel Lane of Stratham,

New Hampshire, had fulfilled his duty: he was the lord of his castle, he dispensed justice and laid down the law within his realm, and he earned that right to do so by providing for his family and dispensing largesse.

Thomas Allen was reverend of the Pittsfield, Massachusetts, Congregational Church for more than forty-six years from 1763 until his death in 1810. After his death, the inventory of his possessions shows a man who enjoyed solid middle-class comfort. He had a minister's lot valued at $8,900,[17] $7,800 of which was in land and buildings. These included a house, barn, and corn house on sixty acres and a "triangle of land" on North Street. In addition he owned a fifty-five-acre meadow (probably) to feed his six pigs, six hogs, sixty-one sheep, a steer, two calves, and a horse. Even these respectable holdings may not have been his entire landholdings, as his last will states, "my sons Thomas, Jonathan, George, Samuel and William have already been given and paid in land-dollars . . . their fair share of the division of the estate."

Allen possessed household items that indicated his relative wealth and social standing, such as fourteen dining plates plus serving platters and much-coveted silver items. His silver included teaspoons, cups, a creamer, teapot, and tankard. Other indications of a socially prominent household were candelabra, a feather bed, a gold pocket watch, and an extensive library.

In eighteenth-century New England, possessions expressed social position as much or more than a bank account. The plates and platters told of a household equipped to entertain. The pocket watch was a gentleman's article, not found on a yeoman. Literacy meant a minimal level of learning mandatory to conduct business; a learned man was a well-read man. A man who had a library was a man of standing.

Domestic Work

My time is not my own but God's.[18]

The experience of the women inside the great house and the regulation house was equally varied. The wife in the regulation house was a laborer, and Mrs. Schuyler was a manager, but both were in charge of production, and for each the products they labored to produce were the property of their husbands. Each was held accountable if there was strife in the family, and both were praised for calm and regulation. They were relied upon for sustenance and subsistence, but their daily routines were very different.

Whether the wife did the work or oversaw it, her efforts were complementary to her husband's and occurred in concert with his. He bought and sold the livestock; she milked the cows. He slaughtered, butchered, and salted the meat; she prepared the food. He planted, plowed, and harvested; she cooked and stored the produce. He may thresh mill and fish, but it all ended in her kitchen or her sewing room. No one was fed or clothed, rested comfortably, or had home spun or food stuffs to trade in the market without her labor. And yet . . .

In the US Censuses from 1790 to 1820, instructions given the census takers specifically prohibited listing "household manufacturing" on the forms; thus, woman's work was unrecorded and rendered invisible by official mandate. She was not paid for her labor, nor could she own the products; moreover, it went (officially) unacknowledged.

Ironically the way we know the most about what she produced was when the marriage broke down. In June 1811, Hannah West's husband Thomas published a notice in the *Vermont Republican*. It stated his wife had "conducted herself in an unbecoming manner, running me in debt and injuring my property."

Since Hannah was quick to respond, we know what she did and what she produced. She accused Thomas of deserting her and taking

> *all my cloth that I had to clothe my family with & all my yarn that I had spinned. He carried away my flax, wool and all the provisions which we raised on our farm last year, which was enough to have supported our family and to have sold to the amount of $200 had it been taken care of in a prudent manner.*[19]

Interestingly, Thomas's complaint was boilerplate, a stock response every discontented husband used regardless of the specifics of his household, but Hannah's complaints are very specific, making it appear her posting more closely reflects the truth.

Small New England farms required huge amounts of manual labor. Everyone worked—men, women, and children—to produce enough to survive and to take to market. Even small New England businesses, inns, taverns, and shops needed both husband and wife working side by side.

Curtis Hale added to his notice:

I do also forbid any payment to her of any debt now due or that shall hereafter become due to me.

Evidently creditors and customers were accustomed to settling accounts with Sally Hale. Perhaps she was the one who could add.

These labors by the wife and on behalf of the husband and family were part of the marriage contract. Failure to perform them or to perform them to the husband's satisfaction was grounds for dissatisfaction and for posting notice of nonsupport.

Once in a while we have a firsthand account of domestic work in the eighteenth century. On a Saturday morning in 1754 a woman wrote to her friend:

I write just when I can get time. My dear you must needs think I can't get much for I have my Sally to tend, and domestic affairs to see to, and company to wait of besides my sewing that I am really rushed.[20]

She was Esther Edwards Burr, and before her marriage she lived on Plain Street in a village called Stockbridge. In Esther's day it was Indian town; birch teepees lined the way. Esther's father was the Reverend Jonathan Edwards, who came to Stockbridge to serve as the second minister to the Stockbridge Congregational Church. It was 1749.

Esther's father was the Jonathan Edwards, author of the intended revival of the Congregational Church referred to as The Great Awakening, a kindly man but a careful father who may have bred more fear than intended. In so serious and pious a household, Esther looked to her soul and sought heaven.

Esther wrote from Princeton, New Jersey. Her husband, Aaron Burr Sr., was co-founder of the college that would be Princeton University. She was twenty-two, he was thirty-eight, and together they had one daughter, Sally. They would have a second child, Aaron Jr., who would become the third vice president of a country not yet formed, an accused and vindicated traitor, a duelist, and a womanizer.

Esther's obligations were similar if not identical to those of any woman in the eighteenth century in a middle-class household: the regulation of the household, including the instructions to her help; the management of the young children; and entertaining that pleased her husband and promoted his interests. "I believe the hardest work I do is entertaining."[21]

"My time is not my own but God's" was not a passing remark but a serious concept and deeply held belief. Domestic work, the regulation of her household, or her "departments" within it, were scared tasks. When on a Sunday she only went to church and then played with her daughter, she was bereft. "O I am ashamed and that justly that I spend my Sabbaths no better."[22]

In her leisure time, when she had any, either as a maid in Stockbridge or a matron in Princeton, she wrote to her dear friend Sarah Prince in Boston. The letters were called their "privacies." Keeping faith with one another and holding each other's confidences Esther considered sacrosanct.

When Esther died at just twenty-five, Sarah wrote, "My dependence in the world for comfort is gone."

The House Next Door

The first foundation of New England's strength and growth was godliness, the next was neighborliness and a firm rock it was to build on.[23]

Before we leave the subject of domestic work, there is a characteristic of society in the pre–Industrial Revolution era not to be overlooked. All members of the community, men and women, were required to be neighborly. To be a good neighbor was tantamount to a sacrament, and it meant more than good manners.

In a time before technology, no single family unit had the manpower to build their house, plant and harvest their crops, or tend their sick without help. Being neighborly was being helpful—hands on helpful.

Intimate Conversation[24]

Let your Dress, your Conversation and the whole Business of your life be to please your husband and make him happy.[25]

A common misconception is that there was no premarital sex in this puritan land. Premarital sex was commonplace. It was encouraged and condoned as long as marriage followed. In this sparsely populated land where survival was labor intensive, a marriage without children was a curse and to be avoided. A pregnant bride in the eighteenth century was devoutly to be desired.

The privacy we enjoy and demand associated with sex—the separate quarters, the closed door, the individual bed—none of these were assumed in the eighteenth century. There was only one room in a regulation house, so both the table of all work and the bed (if one were owned) were in the same room. If there was a bed chamber and if there were a bed in it a number of family members might share it.

Another misunderstanding about eighteenth-century women furthered by the definition of the word puritanical is that they were straitlaced, stuffy, and prudish. Doing her conjugal duty with her lips pursed and eyes shut. Read on.

Thomas A. Foster, in *Sex and the Eighteenth Century Man*, touches also upon the experience of the eighteenth-century woman. While the husband's obligation was to support the wife and hers to serve obediently, "a closer look at what constituted support reveals that sexual and financial obligations were often intertwined."[26] One might add that service included more than preparing meals.

A man, a real man and husband, supported his wife financially, stood between her and the outside world, protected her, and satisfied her sexually. But, for example, the reason for sexual gratification within the marriage was not to express love but to regulate passion. Regulating all baser human emotions was the key to civilizing the community. The church and the men were obliged to so regulate.

Divorce could be sought on the grounds of adultery, consanguinity, desertion, bigamy, and sexual incapacity. Wives complaining against husbands and even asking for a divorce often cited an unsatisfactory sex life. They accused their husbands of being unfit or unnatural. An unfit or unnatural husband was one that either could not adequately fulfill his role as sexual partner or was abusive. Men were solely responsible for ensuring proper sexual behavior in their households. He could demand that his wife be available and willing, and that she not stray, but that did not mean he could do as he pleased. He owed her proper sexual conduct and moderation in his demands.

Again, as with woman's work, it is when the marriage broke down that the most information is available. Divorce records show that the woman expected a fulfilling sex life, and the man took pride in pleasuring a woman.

In Woburn, Massachusetts, Joel Richardson sued his wife for divorce on the grounds of infidelity and treating him cruelly. Susanne testified that she should have filed on the grounds that her husband was incapable. She did not because she meant to spare him the humiliation of making his inadequacy public. Such exposure would have brought his masculinity into disrepute and challenged his standing in the community. Not wanting to ruin his reputation, she decided to poison him instead.

Interestingly, masculine potency was so highly regarded, and the right of a wife to expect sexual satisfaction so central to the marriage contract, that the adultery and poison were forgotten and the case became about Richardson's potency. When he was declared impotent and "unable to procreate," Susanne was triumphant: "He is not a man and God knew it and I knew it."

Homestead in the Context of War

September 21, 1754. Other places are fortifying at their own charge, your people must do so too. . . . Ashley's house is situated best for a garrison for ye protection of Stockbridge and for scouting from too.[27]

The Reverend Thomas Allen was unique: while certainly a man of God, he was also a man of war. He was an early supporter of the Revolutionary War. In 1765 he prayed to "The God of Armies that he would teach their hands to war and their fingers to fight."[28]

When Allen came to the pulpit in 1763, the French and Indian War was just ending. Thirsting for more war was frowned upon. At that early date, Allen's position was radical when compared to those who still believed that colonial resistance would result not in war and separation from England but in compromise. Allen would be proven right, and those who thought the Crown would negotiate were wrong. The minister would fight at Bennington, where it is believed he fired the first shot. All of these property holders—rich, middle class, and poor—were living in the shadow of war.

It was 1754. In the New England countryside, times were rough and, in many ways, colorless. The roads were rutted and often a mere cart-width. When the sun set, the world was dark. The ground was hard, and so was the Church. Reward for a life well spent was anticipated not in this life but only in heaven, and the words discretionary income had no meaning. For three decades, the Colonists would live on a war footing.

The French and Indian War dragged on for nine years (1754–1763). The Revolutionary War began in 1775 and ended in 1783. While the French and Indian War drained the coffers, frightened the settlers, and caused death and destruction, it also prepared the Colonists for the war ahead.

The American troops that fought the British in the Revolutionary War were trained by the British to fight the French. The forts, garrisons, and strong houses built in the 1750s to defend against the French and their Indian allies were used throughout the Revolution.

Knowing the French wanted to march from Canada to Pennsylvania and Ohio, settlers in western Hampshire County (Berkshire County today) feared they were in the enemy's path. Forts were built in North Adams, Williamstown, and Lansborough. The string of forts was interspersed with fortified houses.

In *Stockbridge Past and Present* Electa Jones writes: "Stockbridge lay in the direct route, and it was constantly feared that the French and Indians would be down from the north, and sweep the little mission station before them."

In South County they built "strong houses," or fortified houses. There was Ashley House in Sheffield and two fortified houses in Stockbridge: one on Main Street and one on Prospect Hill Road.

Old Colonel Ephraim Williams back from the building of Fort Mas-sachusetts [North Adams] boxed himself up in his new home on the Hill. Stately and forbidding the castle was really a fort and com-manded the sweep of the valley with the protection of 3 inch plank walls and a well in the basement so that in case of siege those seeking protection would be supplied with water."[29]

Fortified houses were primarily intended to protect small farmhouses and give advance warning of enemy troop movements in the region. There-fore the locations of forts and fortified houses were selected for sight lines so occupants could see long distances. A hill was a prime location. They were spaced so that a warning of impending danger (a gunshot or bell) could be sounded and heard by the next fort or fortification and by the people between. Finally locations were positions they wished to defend: points at which an advance might be stopped, locations from which shots could be fired in many directions.

The post was filled with letters from diligent men in British uniforms distributing money and troops to fortify homes and protect the people in the places designated and to wish the others well. South County was not a priority and received only well wishes. In Stockbridge, Williams's Pros-pect Hill home and on Main Street the Reverend Jonathan Edwards's home were fortified at the owner's expense.

Hornwork, crownwork, bastion, tower, redoubt, and *stockade* are not common words today but in eighteenth-century Berkshire they were. These were descriptors of the parts of forts and fortified houses that were intended to make the structure safe.

Although she was staying in a fortified house on Main Street in Stockbridge, Esther Edwards Burr did not feel safe. Her father, the Rev-erend Jonathan Edwards, was "serene in the face of danger," but Esther wrote, "Oh how distressing to live in fear every moment. I hant had a night's sleep. Since I been here I may say I have had none."[30]

She was younger when she died than many women in the eighteenth century were when they married, but it was not the Indians she need fear, it was smallpox. Nevertheless, she feared one and thought not at all about the other. As the fear grew, she wrote, "This place is in a very defenseless condition—not a soldier in it."[31]

In desperation, Esther "proposed to my father to set out for home next week but he is not willing to hear one word about it so I must tarry the proposed time and if the Indians get me, they get me, that is all I can say, but 'tis my duty to stay."[32]

Women of the eighteenth century did not make their own plans but relied upon their husbands and fathers. Even if they prevailed and their men acceded to their desires, they were not free to travel alone. Esther stayed in Stockbridge, as was her duty, regardless of how she felt. She survived and eventually returned to Princeton, New Jersey, and her two-year-old son, Aaron—the future vice president of the United States. It was there that she contracted smallpox and died at the age of twenty-six in April 1758.

The actions of the men around her may appear to have denigrated her fears. Her father does not heed her wish to be gone. Her husband takes his time in writing. She suffers without sympathy as if her fears are irrational. Just to be clear, there was not a man in plain clothes or a soldier in uniform who was not afraid. This is what Col. Israel Williams wrote to Governor William Shirley:

Hatfield April 12, 1754, Sir, I conclude by this time you are fully informed of the hostile attacks of the Indians, and the mischief done by them in our own frontiers and neighboring governments in one of which they have made terrible waste burning and destroying all before them. . . . It is now open war with us, a dark and distressing scene.[33]

Open war and the battles were just outside the front door, in the dooryard, and across the back field, where they could be seen and heard and present an immediate threat. From 1754 through the Revolutionary War (1775–1783), Shays' Rebellion (1787), and the War of 1812, there were battles in our homeland. Whatever was happening in this country, it was happening in the context of war with all the attending violent death, destruction, and disease.

Chapter 3

The Church

Voted that it is the opinion of the brethren of this church that it is inconsistent with the rules, and the word of God, for Mrs. Deane to join in wedlock with said John Fisk.[1]

One cannot overstate the power and centrality of the Congregational Church in early New England, where villages were theocracies. In *Democracy in America*, Alexis de Tocqueville wrote that there is "no country in the world where the Christian religion retains a greater influence over the souls of men than in America."

In Massachusetts, no town could be incorporated until a meetinghouse was built and a minister hired. It was required that the final division of land include a minister's lot, a school lot, and a town lot (town square) with a meetinghouse.[2]

Regardless of the religion a citizen professed, he was required to buy a pew, to pay taxes to support the Congregational Church, and to attend a service at least once in three months.[3] The same men who served as deacons of the church also were the town selectmen, state representatives, and court judges. Religious services, town meetings, select board meetings, and court sessions might all take place in the meetinghouse.

For women the Congregational Church was contradictory. In the church both men and women were members—equally obliged to obey and equally liable to be punished. Yet the church also, speaking for God Almighty, restricted the role of women in society.

It was Eve who precipitated the fall. It was Eve who brought guilty knowledge into the world and caused humankind to be cast out of Eden.

Woman, for her sins, was to be suspected, monitored, and controlled lest another tragic fall occur.

> *We believe that God at first made man in his own image and entered into a covenant of life with him upon condition of perfect obedience; but that our first parents fell by eating the forbidden fruit thereby bringing sin and ruin upon themselves & all their posterity.*[4]

Church was a place where a woman was a member, and yet it was the place where all the limitations placed upon her were justified. She was to follow the gospel but was not allowed to preach it. She was to be obedient to the precepts but not question, reason, or argue to better understand what was required of her. She could not serve on any committee that shaped the rules or enforced them. Even when they regulated her public and private behavior and placed demands upon her that were almost impossible to meet, she had no way to question the rules.

For example, all her life she was taught to be obedient to the men in her life, and yet she must find a way to repel a man's advances if the coupling would be fornication, adultery, or incest. A maiden was to appear to eschew sexual behavior and be a stranger to sexual gratification at the same time that she was to attract a husband by promising, among other things, conjugal bliss. As a wife she was to live to please her husband and be available to him while finding a way to fend off sexual conduct repellent to her or considered "unclean." She was instructed to be a good neighbor, congenial, and generous to all. At the same time that she was to keep a sharp eye on her husband's money and other resources, she was to be a good businesswoman, who never overpaid or lost in a bargain.

Covenant of the Congregational Church

> *We do now avouch the Lord Jehovah, Father Son, and Holy Ghost, to be our God as far as we know ourselves, heartily giving up ourselves to him & desiring to be His forever; & we promise by divine grace and assistance to walk in all the commandments of the Lord blameless, & we do now subject ourselves to the government of Christ in His Church.*[5]

Subjecting oneself to the government of the Church was not taken lightly, nor was it an easy task. There were the rules for membership, for the conduct demanded of a member, and for punishment when a member failed to behave. In this regard there was absolute equality between the sexes.

In Communion

To be in communion meant to be a member in good standing. Members of the congregation prayed and took communion with their fellow members; they were "in fellowship."

Members were born and baptized into the church and remained for a lifetime. The objective was to "live in grace," with the forgiveness of God and guided by the Holy Spirit. There was also "free grace," richly to be desired, which was forgiveness from God even when undeserving.

After the French and Indian War there was a great influx into Stockbridge, Massachusetts, and Berkshire County generally. The congregations were flooded with recent arrivals who were neither born nor baptized in the church. They became "members by letter." A member by letter was a church member somewhere else and came with a letter as proof.

"That if any person remove from a neighbor church to dwell with us he shall within the space of four months produce a recommendation from the church from which he removed."[6]

That is, he was welcomed because he arrived with a letter from his former church attesting that he left that church in good standing.

In the eighteenth century, there was a revival in the Church. One of the issues debated was baptism. For some, infant baptism was sufficient, but for others a new member had to submit to adult baptism as a sign of sincere faith: proof that one embraced the gospel and did heartily repent. For these revivalists, infant baptism accrued to the spiritual benefit of the parents, who were sentient when it took place rather than the infant who was not.

The Church as Court

She was directed to "mend her ways . . . and return in 14 days and make it known that she sincerely repents her wanton ways."[7]

In the Massachusetts colony, as early as 1636, the "aggrieved" were required to bring their matters before the Church before seeking redress in a civil court. This was a mandatory first step, and complainants prejudiced their cases if they went directly to court. Therefore, the Congregational Church had experience sitting as a court.

The separation of church and state as we know it did not exist. In fact, by precedent if not by law, only if the issue was unresolved in the church would it go to the court. A congregant could bring a grievance related to immoral behavior certainly but also any dispute over land, compensation for work done, or a perceived injury or insult.

The Pittsfield Congregational Church had a unique way of handling these cases. When too many slander cases were brought to the church, rather than adjudicate each one, the church held a "reconciliation." All the members rose and pledged to live in harmony with each other even when there was not perfect agreement between them. Members then filed up and signed the pledge. It was clearly stated that only the men need sign; assent by the women was assumed unless a female dissenter was willing to stand in public and deny it. None did.

A case that would typically come before the church and could not be simply reconciled was a complaint of "criminal conversation," eighteenth-century-speak for "adultery." In 1776, the well-respected Pittsfield citizen and soldier Col. James Easton was accused of criminal conversation by Mr. Dexter of Boston. In the 1700s, this was a suit for damages. A husband, having discovered his wife's infidelity, sued her lover for damage to his property.

Mr. and Mrs. Dexter were guests in the Easton household. While they were not caught in flagrante delicto, Dexter felt their behavior toward one another indicated an excess of intimacy. Of course, in addition, there was, when pressed by him, his wife's admission—a purported admission she refused to repeat.

Colonel Easton was found neither innocent nor guilty. A majority of church members found that there was insufficient evidence to pursue the case. Mr. Dexter returned to Boston without compensation. The real finding may have been that Easton was a well-liked and respected local, and Dexter was a stranger from the city. The telling fact, the comment on the times, may be that the only matter of interest was the contest between the men; no word was recorded about Mrs. Dexter. Did she return to Boston with her husband? Did he divorce her? Did she ever see Easton again? No word is recorded, not even her name.

In 1777 a congregant came before the First Congregational Church "much aggrieved." He was the father of a daughter and he stated the case. There was a gathering of the ladies at the home of a pious and elderly woman. There the wives and daughters gathered to do good works, sew and cook for those less fortunate in the community. The winter of '76 was severe, followed by a late frost. It killed crops and many faced hunger. Good Christians saw it as a duty to "watch over one another faithfully."

So the women gathered and cooked and sewed. When a "goodly stock" of soup and homespun was made up, the women called in the men to load the wagon and transport and distribute the bounty. One among the men was young. He was "too light in manner" for the gravity of the situation. He was not attending to the carrying and loading of the cart. Instead, he was flitting among the young ladies, and he plucked out the ribbon from his daughter's hair. She tried to get it back but he held it high.

The father reported, "[H]e said, where all could hear, 'I will return the ribbon for a kiss.' Whereupon he inveigled a kiss; they sat opposite and he leaned in and also my virgin daughter leaned in and they kissed. The boy prevailed upon her and led her into sinful ways in sight of all the company. I ask that he be admonished and begged to confess and repent."[8]

The old woman at whose house the women met testified to the truth of the father's presentation of the case in every particular. The pastor, as expert witness, declared such behavior prejudicial to the growth of religion in the soul and was "an unhappy influence on our society."[9] The meeting had all the elements of a trial. There was the statement of the charge, testimony, the congregation sitting as jury, and the minister to mete out punishment.

The boy was then asked to confess and repent, but he stood mute. By doing so he risked greater punishment or excommunication. The Pastor demanded, "Speak and save your soul!"

To defend the boy, the girl was forced to speak. She confessed that the kiss was not forced nor was it a first kiss. In fact, with the intention of marriage, they had engaged in sexual intercourse. They wanted to be sure, before committing, that the marriage would be fruitful. While the church and the courts punished fornication, they punished it far less severely if a marriage took place.

Notwithstanding a man's superior position in society, and notwithstanding that a female was the subject of a male, the boy was let off and the girl was held responsible for the unseemly behavior and admonished. She was removed from communion for fourteen days. During that time she was to prepare to admit her sins and "repent before the body." For two weeks she was to "mend her ways and read her Bible." She was directed to study and reflect, listen to her elders, and return in 14 days and make it known that she "sincerely repents her wanton ways."

If all those points were not adhered to, she could be excommunicated. If excommunicated, she could not be married in the church. She could not pray with her family, attend communion, nor in fact be welcomed by the congregation in any way. She would lose society in this life and salvation in the next. The result is not recorded, nor do we know if they ever married or if she was ever tried for the criminal act of fornication.

During the Revolutionary War years, 1775–1783, Pittsfield closed the county courts. Though there were predictions of chaos, Pittsfield did exceptionally well without civil and criminal government. Through it all, five years, order was maintained and the dire threats of lawlessness and impending anarchy were not realized. The church had much experience acting as the judiciary.

Excommunication

All those accepted in communion could also be cast out. The idea of eternal damnation was certainly chilling, but membership offered a more immediate reward. They had carved the village and its church out of the wilderness for the glory of God. They were bound together by isolation without and by the warmth within this church.

William Williams in a letter dated July 1, 1755, described Stockbridge as "a remote corner of the earth." In this vast wilderness, they offered one another fellowship, treated fellow members affectionately, and

William Williams STEPHEN W. GREENFIELD,
WILLIAMS GENEALOGY AND HISTORY, 1847, P.180

watched over one another faithfully. As long as they "walked in the commandments" and were "subject to the government of this church," they had a community and hope to spend eternity in heaven.

They were also cautioned that "Christ judge the world . . . and condemn and doom the ungodly to eternal fire." Therefore, the Reverend Stephen West believed, "We shall know God and God's will through the church, but we must know also his displeasure. Therefore it is our duty to cast out from this body any who offend."[10]

Excommunication, or casting out any who offended, was a weapon of the church—a process by which behavior was regulated and order kept. In eighteenth-century New England, life was not a romp through the countryside; it was a sober stroll through Puritan woods. Life was dangerous, and the Church was a bulwark against the wilderness, against loneliness, and an aid in the struggle to survive.

In return for keeping covenant with the church, it offered its members "our fellowship and communion." In exchange for living under the articles of the covenant, the church would "treat you affectionately and watch over you faithfully and offer up prayers for you." The church protected you in this life and ushered you into heaven.

It was important to have a community "living in harmony" and a place to celebrate the rites of passage from baptism to burial. However, what happened if you did not keep the faith? If you strayed, you could be ousted.

Excommunication was the final, extreme step in a process designed to help you mend your evil ways and bring you back into the fold. Step one was a private chat with the pastor. "No offense in any brother shall be brought before the church till the private steps have been taken." If a private request by the pastor for confession and repentance did not work, the next step was clear.

> *I have taken the steps which the Gospel directs but cannot bring him [the offender] to make Christian satisfaction. Therefore I think it is my duty to complain of him to the church that they may clear him if he be innocent, and if he be guilty bring him to repentance and reformation. Accordingly I lay this complaint before the church for its consideration.*[11]

The complaint could be laid before the church immediately if "the offense be of a public nature or have become a matter of public notoriety," then "the confession shall be made before the church and congregation in full." If you were unwise enough to commit your sins in public, then you stood before all your neighbors, confessed, and repented. You were forgiven if you seemed sincere, but that was not quite enough.

Inherent in the process of confession and repentance was the understanding that you would not sin again. Or, at least, you would not commit the same sin again. The church would formally admonish you not to do so, and if you did not heed the admonishment, then excommunication loomed.

Excommunication simply meant that you could not take communion in the church. In practice, it was more than that. Some who were excommunicated were also rejected by the fellowship in the marketplace and the drawing room. Moreover, to the eighteenth-century man or woman, excommunication put your immortal soul at risk. Excommunication was serious business that could rob you of heaven.

What were the sins that led to excommunication and who were the sinners? According to the "standing rules," sinners included all heads of families who did not worship God with their households; any professor of the faith who married "a profane and immoral person"; any professed follower who practiced dancing, an amusement that was deemed a sinful waste of time; and any who acted in a manner "prejudicial to the growth of religion or an unhappy influence on society."

To take them in order, members who did not regularly attend church were called to account and admonished to mend their ways. If they did not, they were deemed strangers and, like the school truant who is expelled, were excommunicated.

An "unhappy influence" on society is harder to explain. A woman in Sheffield was married to a wealthy and prominent man. She was, nonetheless, admonished on several occasions for being an unhappy influence by breeding discontent and disharmony. She was a demanding woman who was never satisfied. Her conversation was laced with complaints against many people and things. She had private meetings called by the pastor. Once she was admonished publicly for refusing to pay a workman because his work did not please her. She paid up and was not excommunicated. Then the day came when her husband died. The funeral meats were hardly digested when they threw her out with a sigh of relief and good riddance.

A man married a woman who was an "impenitent whore," and a woman married a man who was a "profane and immoral person." Both could confess and repent, but neither could end the marriage, so in a way the sin was continued. Both were excommunicated, and yet the man was readmitted to the church after one year and the woman was not. Why? Because there was, in the pastor's view, "a material difference in the case of a man marrying a woman of immoral character and a woman marrying a profane man. By the law of nature and the written law of God, a woman is more under the influence and control of the man than man is of the woman."[12]

Drinking to excess and promiscuity were deemed sinful wastes of time and behavior prejudicial to the growth of religion, as was dancing. Everyone who went to a tavern sooner or later danced. The liquor fueled the revelry and the revelry led to the dance floor. The only serious cases taken up were when the tavern owner danced and encouraged others to dance, for then he was "discouraging the growth of religion in the soul."

It seems an innocent list by today's standards. Interesting that the social ills we live with and most fear are not mentioned: rape, murder, and acts of terrorism. Were they nonexistent? If so, perhaps life was a romp through the lovely countryside.

Excommunication: The Impenitent Whore

The Church declared their non-communion with Ebenezer Andrus for his crime of marrying an impenitent whore, and continuing himself impenitent.[13]

There it is, a terse twenty-word entry in a church record. The man was Ebenezer Andrus. The woman, nameless, was his wife. Pretty racy for a Congregationalist in 1769. Or is it? Who was this woman and in eighteenth-century parlance what did the twenty words mean?

"Declared non-communion with" meant Andrus was excommunicated. That was the most extreme action the church could take against a member. Excommunication meant he was shunned in this life and lost heaven in the afterlife. Once excommunicated, his children could not be baptized, nor could he or his wife be buried in the churchyard.

In the vocabulary of the eighteenth century, *impenitent* meant just what it does today. Ebenezer married a whore who felt no shame or sorrow, who did not wish to confess, repent, and change her ways.

A whore, on the other hand, might have referred to a prostitute, but equally in eighteenth-century parlance, she might have been a professor of another religion. Which was she? We cannot even find her name; how do we determine the nature of her sin?

Contemporary, first-hand accounts in diaries, letters, and journals are rewarding but rare. The further back in time you research, the fewer letters and journals are available, and the more often they are by the hand of privileged men. No letter survived that was written by Ebenezer Andrus or his wife.

There are contemporary documents that are more formal and more routinely saved. Among these are: vital records; criminal, civil, and probate court records; deeds; tax records; census, birth, baptism, marriage, and death records. These can be found at the New England Historic Genealogical Society as well as in church and town records. Trace the names of husband and wife through these records and find, at least, an outline of their lives. Unfortunately, while the church condemns the woman, it does not find it necessary to name her. Fortunately, we have his name. While there is no will probated for him, and no property owned by him in Berkshire, and no mention of him in the 1771 tax valuations or 1790 census, there is evidence of his marriage.

Also from the New England Historic Genealogical Society, we learn that Andrus was married in Fairfield, Connecticut, in 1746. His wife was "Sarah Sturgis, daughter of Peter." From church records, we learn that they came to Great Barrington and joined the church in 1763. Their daughter, Rebekah, was baptized in the church the following year. In 1766, Sarah died and was buried by the church. Sarah could not have been the "the impenitent whore," first because she was a member of the church and second because he was not excommunicated during their marriage.

Ebenezer remarried sometime between 1766, when Sarah died, and 1769, when he was excommunicated. That marriage record would have contained the name of his second wife and her parents' names. Since the marriage was condemned by the church, it was not performed by the church, and no record was found. If Ebenezer and his second wife had a child, a baptism record might have her name, but since the husband was excommunicated, their children would not be baptized in the church. Though the list of other primary sources is long, none have the name Ebenezer Andrus, and his second wife still has no name.

In 1774, Andrus was readmitted to the church "upon his confession of marrying an unchristian woman." Now we can be certain it was her religious beliefs, not her sexual behavior, that earned her the name "whore."

The resolution of that mystery leaves a larger mystery unsolved. How could Andrus be readmitted to the church? Did his second wife die? Did he leave her? Did he remain married to her while telling the community he was ashamed of the marriage? He could confess that he married an "unchristian woman"; he could repent of it verbally, but how could he change his ways? Must he divorce her?

The answer is in the attitude toward women and the domestic hierarchy. The first concern of the church was that the children be raised properly. Andrus could repent of marrying a woman of a different religion and promise to raise the children in the Congregational church and be forgiven. He could be readmitted because a man's mind was considered stronger than a woman's. His position in the family was more powerful. The rearing of the children in some of the most important ways fell to the man. Therefore by giving his word to live as a good Christian and raise his children in the church, he could be believed and readmitted.

If the situation were reversed, and a woman married an immoral man and was excommunicated, her word would not be accepted. She could not guarantee that she would raise the children in the church because the man would be seen as stronger and more powerful in the family circle. That is the story of the Widow Deane.

Excommunication: The Widow Deane

In Stockbridge, Massachusetts, 1777, Lavinia Higby Deane faced a fearful choice. If she married the schoolmaster, John Fisk, she would be excommunicated from the First Congregational Church of Stockbridge. If she did not marry him, she would give birth—out of wedlock—to his child.

Excommunication meant damnation in the afterlife and isolation in this life. Giving birth to a bastard child was unthinkable for the "good and amiable Widow Deane."

Lavinia was married to her first husband, John Deane, ten years when he died. She gave birth every two years during their marriage. At thirty years old, she was a widow with five children under the age of ten.

John Fisk came to the village late in 1776, hired as a teacher and Keeper of the District Schools. Teachers were paid a respectable 11 pounds 30 per month.[14] Just as important, teachers were highly regarded members of the community. What could have happened that these two respectable people were admonished by the church not to marry?

The deacons of the church met on January 20, 1777, and decided, "It is not consistent with the rules of our holy profession to tolerate any of our members joining in marriage with profane immoral persons. And there is reason to fear that Lavinia Deane a sister of this church is about to join such a one."

They appointed a panel of deacons to investigate the matter. On February 3, 1777, the Widow Deane was formally admonished "to desist from marrying Mr. Fisk." To be called good and amiable meant Lavinia always obeyed the teachings and rules of the church. Yet the church accused Mr. Fisk of swearing. He was heard to say "Damn it" and "Damn it to hell." Searching for a middle ground, Lavinia asked the minister, Dr. Stephen West, whether it would be sufficient to exact a promise from Fisk never to swear again. Lavinia married Fisk in hopes that the promise was enough. It was not.

Fisk's "immorality" was indeed the profanity, but unfortunately, profane meant more than profanity. It meant worldly, not of the Congregation, in fact, not Christian or at least not a good Christian.

On April 25, 1777, Lavinia was excommunicated "until she repents of her manifest sense of wickedness in marrying a profane and immoral man."

How was Lavinia to repent of the marriage? Repent generally meant apologize, cease and desist, but divorce was also sinful. Fisk demonstrated he was a baptized Christian but he never joined the Stockbridge church. There was one option left to them: in 1779, Lavinia Fisk exercised her right to a council hearing. That meant that ministers from other churches would come and sit in judgment of the excommunication and could reverse it.

Dr. West argued that the church could and should admonish against a marriage with an immoral and profane individual and the church should excommunicate all those who ignored an admonition of the church.

The argument was that Fisk was baptized and a member of the same religion as his wife. His profanity was unfortunate but could be repented. Finally the church should not have dominion over whom a member marries. "All talk about only converted people [good Christians] marrying is nonsensical."

Mr. and Mrs. Fisk lost their appeal and continued to be both married and excommunicated. They had no choice but to leave Stockbridge.

It seems an odd story with many unanswered questions. When so many others were admonished or excommunicated and then accepted back into the fold, why not Lavinia? What was the nature of Fisk's immorality and profanity? If he were such a sinner why did the same men who hired him as schoolmaster, acting in the capacity of elected officials, forbid Lavinia to marry him acting in their capacity of deacons of the church? How was he fit to teach their children and not fit to raise hers?

Lavinia Higby[15] was born in Sheffield, Massachusetts, circa 1745. She had two younger brothers, Daniel Jr. and Edward. When her mother died, her father, Daniel, remarried. In 1760 Daniel and his new wife, Christiana, had a daughter, Rachel. A year later, in 1761, Daniel died. Lavinia was sixteen years old and her brothers were thirteen and eleven.

When Daniel Higby's will was probated, his property was valued at 167 pounds: 126 pounds in land and 41 pounds in personal property.[16]

John Fellows,[17] a prominent citizen of Sheffield, was named administrator. In 1762, Christiana was made guardian of Rachel. Evidently she did not want to care for her stepchildren, and Fellows was named guardian to Lavinia, Daniel, and Edward. It may seem sad or disappointing that the stepmother rejected the three children but actually it was to their advantage to be placed in the Fellows household. He was a wealthy and prominent citizen. In his household, Lavinia met men of Fellow's ilk and made a good marriage.

John Deane was a man of substance and of property. Marrying Deane was a step up for the daughter of Daniel Higby, but it was a level union for the ward of General John Fellows and for a maid courted in a General's household. John and Lavinia Deane married in the 1760s, moved from Sheffield to Stockbridge, and joined the Congregational Church.[18] Between 1769 and 1776, Lavinia gave birth to five children: Silas, Stephen, Electra, Lavinia, and Lydia.

The Revolutionary War began in April 1775; in May, John Deane's name appears on the muster roll. He served two months and eight days.

He returned to active service again in October 1775 and re-upped in December 1775.

Serving short periods was commonplace during the war. These were not career soldiers; the war was being fought by farmers. In an agrarian economy, men returned home to sow, to harvest, and to tend the livestock.

In January 1776 Deane was home in Stockbridge and charged drinks at Marsh Tavern on Plain Street. Between January and February 1776 John Deane died. Lavinia paid her husband's tab in late February and signed the ledger book "widow." On her husband's behalf, she turned down the "coat allowance" granted him when he served in December. Many would have needed that coat allowance, but the John Deane estate was valued at 1,081 pounds,[19] almost ten times the value of her father's.

During 1776, the Widow Deane lived in a village with the church at its center. She was by all accounts a good woman, amiable and pretty. When John died, he and Lavinia had been married ten years. She was thirty years old and was left with a good house, an enviable piece of land, and five children under the age of ten.

That year, John Fisk came to the village as a teacher and Keeper of the District Schools. Born in New Milford, Connecticut, he was twenty-five years old. His father, Ebenezer Fisk, served as a captain in the army during the French and Indian War. John was an ensign in Elmore's Connecticut Battalion of the Continental Army during the Revolution. He was promoted and entrusted with a serious responsibility when placed in charge of prisoners. When he resigned his commission, he accepted the position in Stockbridge.

Teaching would not make Fisk wealthy, but the profession was considered to be respectable. The church and town government were one body so Fisk was hired with the blessing of both. Teachers were highly regarded members of the community.

It was arranged that Fisk live in the Deane household. There is no indication who arranged it or why but equally there is no record of an outcry against it. Both were respected members of the community and there was no apparent cause to object. Time passed and Mr. Fisk proposed marriage to the Widow Deane. It was rumored Lavinia was prepared to accept.

When the deacons of the church met on January 20, 1777, and decided, "It is not consistent with the rules of our holy profession to tolerate any of our members joining in marriage with profane immoral persons,"[20] it was a shock. How could it be that just months after hiring Fisk as a good man able to teach and care for their children, he was unfit to marry the Widow Deane?

This was a famous case. The repercussions went beyond the impact on Lavinia Deane and John Fisk; it went to the core of church doctrine. The case was carefully documented and there were published arguments years after.

The pastor was Stephen West of the First Congregational Church of Stockbridge, Massachusetts. The grounds on which West approached the widow were these: rumor had it that the widow intended to marry. She had chosen a man who was not a member of the Stockbridge church. Further there were children in the household who had been baptized in the church.

Apparently the man, John Fisk, was a Christian but had never been "desirous of being examined as to his qualifications for church membership and fellowship." That was suspicious, and there had been complaints against him—against his character and his language.

Furthermore, the widow was a woman of property. She had a large house and working farm on the west side of town "near the Great Pond."[21] It was thought she might be vulnerable to one wishing to take advantage, and it would be the responsibility of her church to guard her.

The Reverend West approached her privately. He sat with the Widow Deane to determine the facts and her intentions. He told her openly and clearly that "we believe it unlawful for professors of the faith to marry profane and immoral persons."

The widow did not understand. She knew the meaning of the words: profane meant unconverted, non-Christian, stranger to the word. It was unlawful for a Christian to marry a non-Christian. Immoral referred to indulging in any unsanctioned behavior such as taking the Lord's name in vain—swearing.

She freely admitted that she was contemplating marriage to John Fisk; however she believed Fisk was a Christian. The pastor opined that she was a sister of the church, which was bound to protect and defend her. She thought him a good Christian man, but the minister asked, "Might it may be that in an effort to woo and win you, he has been careful to show only his best side and not all his parts. In short you could be deceived." The widow said, "I pray it is not so."

Reverend West promised to appoint a committee to investigate the question, and asked the widow not to marry John Fisk until the deacons rendered an opinion. He told her, "We require it of one who is under the care and protection and also the watchful eye of this church." "I am a sister of this church. I have been faithful to the sacraments," she replied. "We do not doubt that you are an amiable woman."

What seemed the most difficult to understand is that Fisk was hired as a schoolmaster, vetted as it were by town and church. But the minister simply maintained that they too might have been deceived.

"We ask only that you wait and we will report to you. We mean no harm to Mr. Fisk; we mean only to *protect you*, a sister of this church. He is not a member of this church; our obligation is not to him."

As they parted the minister said, "Go now and stay on the path of righteousness." It was tantamount to an admonishment to wait.

Reverend West now had a clear obligation to appoint a committee to investigate the morality and the Christianity of Fisk before she could be admonished. They appointed a panel of deacons to investigate the matter. One of the deacons judging the case was a debtor to the estate of John Deane. That may seem ill-advised, but the body of deacons was a small one and many in town owed money to the Deane estate.

Witnesses came before the committee who heard Fisk using certain expressions. The minister assured them that they would be absolved for using the obscenities if they were only quoting, but they must be precise.

One witness heard Fisk say, "Damn it; God damn it, and I swear to God."

"Might he have been swearing at you?"

The witness demurred.

"Was there not a rumor that you were taking wood from the school-house supply?"

The witness demurred.

Another witness passed Fisk's sleigh and heard him swear at his horses and say, "Damn them to hell." Furthermore it was on the Sabbath. The witness was going to church; Fisk was not.

A woman testified that she told Fisk the deacons may decide against him and bar the marriage to Widow Deane. Mr. Fisk responded, "[N]ot the pastor, not the deacons, nor all the devils in hell, shall prevent me and the Widow Deane settling together."

A deacon asked, "Is it your testimony that he was challenging the authority of the church?"

Witness, "I do say it."

The deacons conferred and determined that "the particular expressions that came from the mouth of Mr. Fisk, and were here testified to, are ones never known to come from the mouth of any but those who are immoral and profane in character."

The deacons reported to West, who said, "They [the profanities] are reminiscent of the camp, and we must take into account that Fisk was very recently a captain in the militia."

What weighed more heavily was that he was heard to swear often during a period of time when he was trying to recommend himself to the good opinion of the widow. Further, he used unguarded speech when his duties as schoolmaster should have put him on his guard with respect to his conduct and speech. The other thing that weighed against him was that he was "among us" too long a time not to have applied for church membership, and too short a time to be heard swearing on three occasions. "His mouth was filled with profanity and threats and that constitutes a profane and immoral character."

The most severe was his threatening the authority of the church. The deacons came to a unified decision: the church must stand inviolate and revered.

On February 3, 1777, the Widow Deane was formally admonished: "We admonish Mrs. Deane to desist from marrying Mr. Fisk." If she ignored the admonition, she would be excommunicated. Excommunication meant eternal damnation not only for herself but also for her children.

To be called good and amiable meant the Widow Deane had always conformed to the teachings of the church and obeyed the rules. Yet of what had the church accused Mr. Fisk? Fisk had been heard to say "I swear" and "Damn it" and most unfortunately, "Damn it to hell." Lavinia thought it should be sufficient to tell the minister, Dr. Stephen West, that she had exacted a promise from Fisk never to swear again. Dr. West did not agree.

Within the week, Fisk was in the tavern shouting, "If they try and stop me, the pastor, the deacons or I shall die."

Others tried to calm him, "You are too hasty in your speech."

Fisk replied, "By the living God it shall be so."

In an effort to marry in the church and to marry without Lavinia being excommunicated, Fisk went to West. He repented his unguarded speech and begged for pardon. The minister refused him, saying it had gone beyond private confession and repentance. Fisk then offered to stand before the entire congregation, confess, and repent. Again he was denied because he was not a member of the congregation.

A man with a healthy temper, Fisk demanded, "Say the worst that is known of me: has any magistrate ever found me guilty of a crime? Has any tribunal ever found me guilty of sacred or civil disobedience? Was I found to be a lewd person, a drunk, a cheat, a liar, an enemy to this country?"

In fact Fisk could demonstrate he honored service for an extended period in the first year of the war. Further he had been given the unenviable task of escorting prisoners to Albany. En route people were generous in offering the American soldiers food and a roof for the night but refused to feed the prisoners. Fisk, in his turn, refused to eat unless the prisoners were fed, and therefore all survived the march to Albany. For their increased comfort, he allowed them to walk unfettered. He explained to his charges that they must stay in rifle range. If they moved out of range, he would kill them. If they were orderly and remained within range, they would not be shackled. He lost just one prisoner. That one escaped, but he lost none to injury or disease.

The minister could only repeat that Fisk was openly profane in speech and that was a sign of immoral character. Fisk pressed for a remedy, and West continued to deny there was one. Finally West said, "You are in an unconverted state." Being in an unconverted state meant that Fisk was neither a Christian nor a member of the Congregational Church; it meant he had not been baptized. Therefore the Church was powerless to provide a remedy.

Although Fisk was baptized in a Congregational church in Connecticut and could prove it, nothing he said or did impressed West. Being baptized as an infant did not count in West's opinion "because it was not your choice and you were in an unknowing state."

It may seem that West was being unduly difficult and arbitrarily closed the door on Fisk, but it was a delicate time in the Congregational Church, and one of the issues was whether adult baptism was a requirement of true faith.

Again Fisk offered to subject himself to the authority of West and his church, to be baptized if necessary to "come into grace" and be married in the Widow Deane's church. But he was condemned and denied any avenue for redemption. It was up to the widow, and that good and amiable woman was about to defy the church.

Sometime between February 3 and April 25, Lavinia married Fisk in spite of the admonition. Fisk's certainty and his rage, that he intended to marry and refused to be prevented by the church, may have convinced her. Or perhaps the deciding factor was that she was pregnant. Since the baby, John Deane Fisk, was born November 4, 1777, Lavinia had become pregnant and was admonished not to marry the father at about the same time.

They could not marry in the Stockbridge church nor any other Congregational church that knew of the excommunication. One church would honor the ruling of the other. So where did they marry? Fisk was from Connecticut and served in the army in King's County, New York (Columbia County today). In one place or the other they found a way to marry.

On April 25, 1777, Lavinia was excommunicated because "she manifest her sense of wickedness in marrying a profane and immoral man until she repents of it." Her sins were threefold: she married a profane and immoral man, she exposed her innocent Christian children to his evil influence, and she challenged the power of the church by defying its admonition.

Others excommunicated for dancing and drinking and lying, for not keeping the Sabbath, exercised the right and the duty to confess and repent and swear most solemnly to change their ways, whereupon they were allowed back into the church. Mrs. Fisk was offered no avenue to confess her sins, most sincerely repent of them, and return to the fold.

One reason was that she could not "mend her ways." That is, she could not undo a marriage that was consummated. Therefore she was offered no way to return to the church, to the light of the word, and the warmth of fellowship.

However, there was one possibility for her salvation. In 1779 Lavinia Fisk exercised her right to a council hearing. That meant that ministers from other churches would come and sit in judgment of the excommunication and could reverse it, similar to a court appeal. She was, in a sense, putting the church and its decision on trial. It was unlikely to endear her to the minister and deacons of the church. The congregation, however, gave its "full-throated approval."

By the time the council met, Lavinia had given birth to a second Fisk child.[22]

In convening the council, Dr. West was cautious to select the ministers who would sit in judgment. In theory both parties had a right to choose, but the Fisks were at a disadvantage not knowing many ministers. West wanted to make certain the ministers chosen were as conservative as he. There was a great divide in the church at this time. Issues such as adult baptism and the right of the church to approve or disapprove of martial partners were hotly contested. On the first two issues West intended to select ministers who would agree with his views. A third issue, communion, was one he intended to omit from the proceedings.

The conduct and the discipline of the church in excommunicating one of its members have excited attention and the church has agreed to take council on the subject, but not without restrictions. We are sensible that this case is of such a nature as might seem to bear a relationship to any controversy respecting the terms of communion, that is, the terms, if any, on which a person profane and immoral and visibly impenitent might be admitted to the church. We consider ourselves possessed of satisfactory light, and do not think it necessary to ask for council on this subject.[23]

Fisk wasn't having it. "I came to you and asked to stand before this congregation, confess and repent and you denied me on the grounds that I was not, and could not become, a member, therefore the terms of admission must be a part of the deliberations of this council."

The minister took the position that they did not admit to the church the enemies of God just as "Our Lord Jesus cast out the enemies of God from the temple." Fisk insisted therefore that they prove he was an enemy of God. Because there would have been no basis for the admonishment of the Widow Deane if the church had not "characterized me as immoral and profane, a stranger, an enemy; if I am not unconverted, there were no grounds to admonish my wife not to marry me."

Fisk had certainly derailed West's plan. Who could be accepted in communion became the first issue taken up. Whatever Fisk had hoped to accomplish by putting himself on trial, however, he was disappointed. The deacons lined up witness after witness who testified that Fisk did not observe the Sabbath and did swear frequently.

There did seem to be a predisposition to find Fisk guilty. Some testimony could clearly be understood in a fairer light.

My grandson couldn't read. I set him to reading the Bible, but he could not. I feared he never would but the School Master, Mr. Fisk, said the words in the Bible were too far removed from the everyday speech and he got another book—he called it a reader—and that book had simple words, see, look, jump, run, horse and such. Soon my grandson could read that book. But I was uneasy in my mind and wanted to be sure that boy could someday read his Bible. So I said that to the School Master, and he said, "By the living God, I won't quit until your grandson reads every word of any book he wishes."[24]

To say "by the Living God" was unacceptable speech, but the larger question was: had Fisk degraded the Bible? The witness could not answer:

I don't rightly know what removed means. It may or may not be a bad thing. I wouldn't like it to mean the Bible was removed from our everyday lives, it isn't and shouldn't be . . . but it might mean above

48

the everyday, better than common talk, which I would say that it is. And the swearing, well, he said it with a smile. Not like he was cursing when angry, but maybe seeking strength as we all do from God Almighty. He said it right enough, but I just want to say, he was smiling. And I want to say my grandson reads now—the Bible and all. I don't want to appear ungrateful to the School Master because that boy reads now.[25]

Moving to the central issue, Dr. West argued that the church had both the right and the obligation to admonish against a marriage with an immoral and profane individual. West's contention was that, "[i]n all our civil and temporal concerns, we are to consult the glory and good of the Kingdom of Christ."[26] The church had authority over all matters, and further the church had to excommunicate all those who ignored an admonition of the church because that challenged church authority.

The argument on the other side was made by Joseph Huntington of Connecticut. It was that Fisk was baptized and a member of the same religion as his wife so not profane or an enemy of Christ. His immoral behavior, swearing, was unfortunate but not so unusual. Finally, the church should not have dominion over the choice of a mate. Marriage "has nothing of the spiritual in it but is merely a civil and social connection . . . all talk about only converted people [good Christians] marrying is nonsensical." Here was the clear argument that, in the not too distant future, would lead to a separation of church and state in the new republic.

On Fisk's behalf, Joseph Huntington, his Connecticut minister, asked the assembly: "Is it not possible for a good man, a Christian man, to sin?"

The answer was yes.

"Do we cast out all who have sinned?"

The answer was no.

"If we did there would be no one left in fellowship. So why do we not forgive Fisk and take in him and his wife?"

However rational the arguments on Fisk's behalf, West had chosen his judges well. Mr. and Mrs. Fisk lost their appeal. They continued to be both married and excommunicated. The question is: why did they not forgive Fisk and take him in?

Further questions to ponder: If he was immoral and profane, why hire him and continue to pay him to teach their children? If it was merely his profanity and the fact that he did not ask to join the Stockbridge Church, the remedies seem simple. There were roads to redemption as well as a path to entering the church. Was there another reason the church was opposed to the marriage? As the story unfolds, it becomes clear that more than religious principles motivated the church; money and politics played a part.

Money

When John Deane died, his estate was valued at 1,081 pounds: 381 pounds in personal property, and 200 acres valued at 700 pounds. That is an estate worth about $2 million in today's dollars. On the property were a thirteen-room house, a shop, two barns, the cellars, the dooryard, and a cistern. The property was divided as follows:

Wife: 64 acres and 5 of 13 rooms and the shop
Silas: 38 acres and 2 rooms
Stephen: 21 acres and 1 room
Electra: 22 acres and 1 room
Lavinia: 25 acres and 2.5 rooms
Lydia: 20 acres and 1.5 rooms
All shared the use of water, the cellars, two barns, dooryard, all entrances to the house, and the cistern.

These were the ages of the family members at the time of probate: Lavinia, thirty-three; Silas, eleven; Stephen, nine; Electra, seven; Lavinia, five; and Lydia, three. The wife inherited approximately 20 percent, and at least 80 percent of the inheritance went to the minor children.

Lavinia was a trustee, and when she married, Fisk assumed the role. The matter for him to attend to included collecting and paying debts and establishing the guardianship of the children. The proceedings dragged on for seven years before guardianship was ultimately established.

According to the law of the land in 1777, on the day Lavinia married, the property that she inherited became the property of her new husband.

The community's investment in who the Widow Deane married was significant. There may have been many young men, sons of the deacons, for example, who had an eye on the huge property on the west side of town. The man who married her gained 20 percent of the estate, and the guardian of the children, 80 percent. In 1785, they took her children.

One of the deacons who first sat in judgment, John Bacon, and who owed the estate money, became guardian. The co-applicant for guardianship was Timothy Woodbridge. The argument before the court was that the children were baptized in this church, therefore, it was the obligation of the church to see to their welfare, protect their souls, and assure they were raised as Christians, a thing Fisk could not do. They won their case standing before judges who were also deacons. By the time they were taken from their mother, Silas was eighteen; Stephen, sixteen; Electra, fourteen; Lavinia, twelve; and Lydia, ten. Fisk fought the church and fought in court. He lost in both places. Soon afterward, Lavinia, Fisk, and their four children left the village; the Deane children remained.

The Reverend Joseph Huntington, the Connecticut minister who argued for Lavinia and John Fisk, was asked if he hated the church. He replied, "No, I love this church and all it stands for and the chaos it stands against. But it is as if a loved one is out of health, I don't stop loving him, but I must do all I can to nurse him back to health."

Nowhere, Yet Everywhere Present

Lavinia disappeared from this story. Apparently this was a duel between men. No one spoke to her and no one spoke of her. It is possible she did not attend the council. Her absence was a function of her world. Her absence was the most important information about the nature of the world in which she lived.

Furthermore, any explanation of what motivated the actions of the parties involved would not include her. She will not appear again for the next several pages. How is it that she disappears during a process that so affected her life? That is central to understanding the eighteenth-century woman. The women were not actively involved in that which ruled over every part of their lives.

It may be fair to ask: Did this ever have anything to do with her as an individual? Was it an avenue to him? Was she the poster child for the Great Awakening to highlight, explain, and defend the new precepts? Possibly, but she did commit one sin. Any of her sisters would be punished for committing this sin, the sin of all women since Eve. She defied the direct order of a man.

Politics

While the flexibility of his understanding and acceptance of worldly matters may surprise, no position the Reverend Thomas Allen took was as startling as his stand against the Constitution of the Commonwealth and his demand that all courts in Berkshire close until another constitution was written. It was a position sufficiently radical to attract attention even during the Revolutionary War.

During the war, Allen led Berkshire County residents to take a most unique position: They joined the Massachusetts regiments and fought against Great Britain at the same time that they effectively seceded from Massachusetts. It all started with a letter.

In the period between being Colonists and becoming citizens of a new nation, there was, naturally, confusion. In May 1775 the Massachusetts Convention wrote John Adams, Massachusetts representative to the Continental Congress: "We are happy in having an opportunity of resting our distressed state before the representative body of the Continent."[27]

The problem was, if the king and the king's men no longer ruled the province, who did? Without an established government, how were they to enforce laws, pursue civil claims, finalize contracts, buy and sell land, or maintain order?

In answer to the letter, John Adams took the position that Massachusetts should at once cease to function as a colony and call a state convention. The people should elect delegates to the convention, and those representatives chosen by the people should establish a state government. When he laid this before the Continental Congress, he expressed the belief that all colonies should do the same. The members demurred. At that early stage, many thought they were fighting for better conditions in the colonies, not to become an independent country. Therefore, Adams was out-voted.

On June 9, 1775, they answered that "the inconveniences arising from the suspension of the powers of government are intolerable. [An Assembly should] govern according to its Provincial Charter." That left the extant laws in place, the general court in power, and its local courts of law in operation. No one liked continuing under the provincial charter, but they liked lawlessness less. On June 19 the Massachusetts Convention voted to accept the recommendation of the Continental Congress.

By November 1775, the Continental Congress shifted position, and when they received a similar plea from New Hampshire, they answered:

Recommended that New Hampshire call a full and free representation of the people . . . and establish a form a government as, in their judgment, will best produce the happiness of the people and most effectively secure the peace and good order . . . during the present dispute between Great Britain and the Colonies.[28]

New Hampshire, and every state after that, received from the Continental Congress the "Adams" recommendation; it served to fan the flames in Berkshire County.

In December 1775, in town meetings, two villages—Lenox and Pittsfield—explicitly rejected the Massachusetts Convention's decision and denied the state's civil authority in Berkshire. Lansborough followed suit and voted to "Make manifest to the General Court that this town disapprove of [state] laws until a new Constitution shall be sent to us."[29] The Constitutionalists of Berkshire County were born.

Under the leadership of Pittsfield minister Thomas Allen, Berkshire County refused to follow the provincial laws and refused to seat the civil or criminal courts in Berkshire unless and until there was a new constitution. With the exception of Hancock and Alford, every town voted to eschew state government. Berkshire closed the courts and "explicitly forbid" its representatives "to assist in legislation under the current laws." Berkshire had declared war on both Great Britain and Boston. It was on its own.

Lenox JOHN WARNER BARBER, *HISTORICAL COLLECTIONS*, 1841, P. 183

Some historians have called Berkshire County's position in 1775–1780 contradictory. Allen believed their position was absolutely consistent. The Constitutionalists maintained that the Bill of Rights superseded any advice from the Continental Congress. They believed that the underlying principles of the Revolution and practical politics must be inexorably linked, and therefore, a new constitution assuring the rights of the people was mandatory. Otherwise, the war would be a useless exercise, and the people, even if they won the war, would be no better off.

Allen and the Constitutionalists went further. The new constitution must be acceptable to the people. He wrote, "The people are the fountain of power." This was a radical belief indeed. Hierarchy was accepted. Religious beliefs accepted the ultimate supremacy of God, and government came not from the people but from God. The limits of government were proscribed by the "best of men"—those God chose for positions of power. A government formed by the people and limited only by the law to which all were equally subject was unknown. Individuals in Berkshire who were anti-Constitutionalists were most often the ministers and deacons of the churches, and those who had held power under the old regime. Reverend West in Stockbridge was an anti-constitutionalist, as were his deacons. So how was it that a Congregational minister, Thomas Allen, became leader of the Constitutionalists? Let Allen explain in his own words:

*December 1775, To the Representative Body sitting at Watertown:
Only an unalterable attachment to liberty and an invincible love of
civil rights and religious liberty induced us to add to your burdens
[and demand a new constitution with] civil and religious liberty
[that] no length of time will corrupt as long as the sun and the moon
shall endure.*[30]

It was a laudable principle but not as persuasive of the old adage "Never break another man's rice bowl." The Constitutionalists were threatening the power positions and incomes of many in Berkshire County. The men who were judges in the courts were also deacons of the church. They had been benefiting financially from their positions for many years and hoped to continue to do so. They planned to retain their seats of power, and so they were emphatically anti-Constitutionalist.

Fisk was a vocal Constitutionalist; the minister and deacons were anti-Constitutionalists. For the anti-Constitutionalists, secular power was divinely ordained. For the Constitutionalists, power rose up from the people.

More than harboring a political disagreement, the Constitutionalists threatened the livelihood of the anti-Constitutionalists. To threaten the provincial laws and demand a constitution threatened their jobs.

Divinely ordained or not, as a purely practical matter, it was anti-Constitutionalists who sat as the judges, magistrates, and representatives to the general court (legislature) in Boston, and they were compensated for it. If the provincial laws were set aside, they would lose their jobs and salaries.

The same people held the positions or rotated between the positions of selectman, representative, judge, and deacon. Noting the small number of town leaders, many scholars called the Stockbridge village government an oligarchy. This is what and who Fisk stood against.

Fisk might have been at odds with the church leaders on another basis, and it might have been sufficient to stop him joining the church when he arrived in Stockbridge.

The Stockbridge leaders were anti-Constitutionalists, and anti-Constitutionalists were Federalists. Returning soldiers had a "grievous complaint against the Federalists who numbered among their ranks few who had seen active service."[31]

Perhaps the issues of the Great Awakening—such as the necessity for adult baptism, the right of the church to forbid a marriage, or the question of whether marriage was a civil right or a religious union—were academic compared to those of money and power. Even if the question of whether marriage was a civil or religious union was "the most interesting test of the relation between civil and religious authority in Revolutionary Berkshire,"[32] still the underlying and greatest truth was that in New England, religion and politics were inexorably linked. That rich mix ruled over women's lives.

For five years that powerful combination ruled everyone's life in Berkshire County. During that time, under the Reverend Allen's leadership, Berkshire County was a mini-state. It rode out its divorce from Boston, and triumphed. Early in the process Boston ignored the Berkshire rebellion. Anti-Constitutionalists repeatedly communicated their concerns, and Bostonians were forced to acknowledge the problem. They tried to repackage the provincial laws, removing the king's name and leaving the laws otherwise unchanged. Berkshire held fast. In the end Berkshire forced a state constitution, approved by the people, and savored the victory.

In Berkshire County, Massachusetts, the Constitutionalists won. John Fisk collected a mixed bag: He lost some of what he hoped to gain in his marriage, but he left Berkshire County with the wife he had chosen and all four of his children. In Berkshire County, Lavinia Deane Fisk lost everything—her home, her church, and five of her nine children.

Chapter 4

The Village

*Another proof of the goodness of the country [air] is the prolific
behavior of the female sex among us. Barren women beget and
bring forth sons. Women that have left off for 5, 6, 7,
and 9 years, begin anew.*[1]

In a sparsely populated world dependent on manual labor, promoting
prolific behavior was high praise for village life.

On March 28, 1767, William Williams—a Pittsfield town selectman,
governmental leader, and wealthy man—wrote a letter to his brother-
in-law, Nathaniel Dickenson in Deerfield. He described his village, and
while not all residents felt as Williams did, even if a respectable percentage did, Pittsfield, Massachusetts, was a paradise.

Dickinson was ill, and Williams began by expressing his "hearty sympathy on the state of your health."[2] However, this was not a mere sympathy note. Williams had a solution to Dickinson's suffering: move to
Pittsfield.

*Languor, sickness and excruciating pain where my portion while I
chose or rather was obliged [to live elsewhere]. Since my removal to
this place, I challenge any man . . . to compare with me for health
or freedom from pain. . . . And never have I but two half days been
absent from public worship in fourteen years.*[3]

The two half days when Williams was absent from worship were due
not to illness but to the weather conditions. Passing over a description of

a Berkshire winter, Williams explained that the promise of health was due to the "temperature and goodness of the air."

And that was not all. Pittsfield promised longevity: Fewer people died in Pittsfield, or, as Williams put it, "[T] he records of the Probate office avail that in near about six years, [fees] have not amounted to ten pounds to the judge."

Move to Pittsfield—and if sick, you will get better; when better, you will not die. But that's not all folks: At the other end of the life continuum, you will have more children. "Another proof of the goodness of the country [air] is the prolific behavior of the female sex among us. Barren women beget and bring forth fourth sons. Women that have left off for 5, 6, 7, and 9 years, begin anew."[4]

Between life's beginning and the postponement of the end, life in Pittsfield couldn't be better. The women "feel frisky" and "give their men a hearty welcome when they return home from work." Perhaps that accounted for the increase in births. "The men are alert and perceive the difference of the soil . . . it would yield more than they were acquainted with." Better and better: "No man or woman of but common understanding that ever came and got settled among us wishes themselves back."

If health, longevity, abundant children, good soil, and frisky wives didn't sell Dickinson on the move to Pittsfield, perhaps wealth would. Williams wrote, "I fill this paper with instances of growth in estates in just a few years." He recounted tales of men who arrived in Berkshire County with "but 5 pounds" and achieved wealth. Among them was Colonel Ashley, "who came to Sheffield with less money than your minister carried to Deerfield and is now worth more than any man in our county." In Pittsfield, "Goodrich, Brattle, Bush, Hubbard, Crowfoot and Ensign strictly speaking were in debt when they came [and now are among the richest men in Pittsfield]."

Williams ends with the hope that Dickinson will move to Pittsfield for his own sake and to make his sister [Williams's wife] happy.

Women in the Wilderness

Is there a less hyperbolic description of a woman's life in Berkshire? Actually at least two women associated with early Berkshire earned more power and prestige than commonly granted an eighteenth-century woman. First, general court granted the right and responsibility to complete the settlement of Poontoosack[5] to a woman at a time when proprietors were invariably men.

Proprietor Col. John Stoddard died in 1748. His widow, Madam Prudence Chester Stoddard, was authorized by the general court in Boston "to act for her minor children in disposing of the seventeen rights which remained unsold and bringing forward the settlement."[6] That meant she had a huge property to dispose of,[7] and it also meant she had the responsibility to bring people into the area—fallow land was anathema. It did not mean that she was a resident of Berkshire. Madam Prudence was a woman of power and property, one of the Connecticut river gods by marriage, if not descent.

The life of the first female settler was strikingly different. Among the pioneers who settled Poontoosack (Pittsfield, Massachusetts today) were Solomon Deming and his wife Sarah. Sarah Deming was the first white woman to arrive in the new territory.

This monument is erected to commemorate the heroism and virtues of the first female settler and the mother of the first white child born within its limits. Surrounded by tribes of hostile Indians she defended in more than one instance, unaided, the lives and property of her family, and was distinguished for the courage and fortitude with which she bore the dangers and privations of a pioneer life.[8]

What did she do to earn the accolade? We can only guess; the inscription is all we have. It was the summer of 1752. In two years the French and Indian War would commence in earnest. There were bands of Indians hostile to settlers in the area. A log cabin was poor proof against intruders, but there was a door that could be closed and bolted. There were windows without glass but with shutters that latched. What did the goodwife do beyond closing a door and shouting "Go away!"? We will never know exactly, but whatever it was she was credited with repeatedly defending home and family in the lonely wilds.

That same summer Nathaniel Fairfield arrived with his new wife, Judith. The trip from Westfield to Poontoosack was his "honeymoon." His household goods were stacked on a dray (heavy cart) pulled by a yoke (pair) of oxen. The trip was approximately thirty-eight miles through woodland. The Fairfields found their way by following a blazed trail (marked trees). A trip that took two hours in the nineteenth century and forty minutes in the twentieth took the Fairfields three days. There was nothing remarkable about their travel experience. What was remarkable for the Fairfields as for all the pioneers was that they made it at all.

By November 1752, Sarah had a female companion and Madam Prudence relinquished her responsibility by selling her holdings to William Williams. She addressed a letter to "The Honorable Timothy Dwight and other Gentlemen Commissioners" to inform them of the sale. "Colonel Williams having already been at Poontoosack in order to bring forward a settlement, and intending to return early the next spring to reside permanently."[9]

The Land—An Overview

Wild and untamed, Berkshire County was the westernmost point in Massachusetts, the farthest from the seat of government in Boston, and the western tip of New England. It was a place apart: separated from other Massachusetts towns and cities by distance and by a ring of mountains. Everything necessary—a mill, a home, a garden, a government body—had to be created.

Reflecting upon the establishment of Berkshire County, Mark Hopkins wrote in 1844 that Berkshire was peculiar in its isolation, and singular in that most of its business was conducted with New York rather than within its own state of Massachusetts: "[B]etween us and our fellow citizens in the eastern part of the state, there is a perceptible difference."

Berkshire's isolation from the rest of Massachusetts was made manifest in another way. The Pilgrims landed at Plymouth in 1620; Springfield was incorporated in 1636. It took less than twenty years for settlers to move from the Atlantic, 122 miles inland. It took nearly another hundred years for settlers to find their way the next thirty miles from Springfield to

Berkshire County. It was 1733 before the first village in Berkshire County was incorporated.

In 1761 there were four incorporated towns in Berkshire County. In order of incorporation, they were Sheffield, 1733; Stockbridge, 1739; Great Barrington, 1761; and Pittsfield, 1761. The first census was taken in 1790, so the following population figures for 1761 are approximate: Sheffield, 1,047; Stockbridge, 217; Great Barrington, 531; and Pittsfield, 418. (New Marlboro, with a population of approximately 714, was identified as a separate district in 1759 but not incorporated as a town until 1775.) That is just under 3,000 people living in approximately 927 square miles of land and 20 square miles of waterway along a north-south strip approximately 25 miles long.

There were obstacles to travel into the county, and there were obstacles to travel within the county. There were ridgelines bisecting Berkshire, and rivers, marsh, and wetlands making travel difficult. The topography created more than natural obstacles to travel—they created psychological limits. There were myths and legends. When the sun set over the eighteenth century, the world was dark, an impenetrable black. Mist rising over wetlands and swampy areas gave rise to tales of evil spirits. There were areas that settlers were warned not to travel at night lest one be—literally—spirited away. There were rock outcroppings and mountain crags never to be approached in safety for fear they were haunted by angry ghosts. These dangers were mythical, but in the wilds, there were real dangers. Wolves were plentiful and ravenous enough so that there was a bounty paid for killing wolves in Berkshire until 1775. There were Indian raids—a by-product of the French and Indian War. Laying aside superstition, Berkshire settlers were isolated in a very beautiful but dangerous land.

If women were the delicate flowers they were purported to be, weaker than men in mind and body, the land would have killed them all. Instead, what they needed they had to produce, and women worked side by side with men for the survival of the family.

Every home was a farm or at least a residence with extensive gardens and a cow, pig, goat, or duck. The first public works projects established roads and mills. For the grain they could not grind themselves, the clothes

Sheffield   JOHN WARNER BARBER, *HISTORICAL COLLECTIONS*, 1841, P. 92

they could not make themselves, the products they could not create, wagons were dispatched to Hudson to purchase goods from boats coming up and down the Hudson River from New York City and Albany.

It was a hard life, and yet the population in the first ten years of Berkshire life grew at a greater rate than the populations of towns to the east. Sheffield went from 1,047 to 1,318; Stockbridge from 217 to 752; Great Barrington, 531 to 961; Pittsfield, 418 to 1,132; New Marlborough, 714 to 1,087; and four other settlements emerged. The Berkshire population almost doubled, from less than 3,000 to almost 6,000. The next ten years would bring greater growth. Why?

Notwithstanding the arduous travel, the isolation, and the seemingly hardscrabble life, there was a great reward in store for those who made the journey to Berkshire County. The same statistic used to describe an isolated, underpopulated and undeveloped region describes the reward: 2,900 people in 950 square miles. In exchange for any and all difficulties, there was land: lots of land. Berkshire was one of the last best places in Massachusetts to find large tracts of available land, and so the settlers came to get it.

Forming an Incorporated Village

They came for the land. From Plymouth Rock to Concord Bridge, for 155 years, the first settlers moved west in search of land. In an agrarian-based economy, land was survival.

One hundred and thirteen years after the landing at Plymouth, the westernmost part of New England was the last place in Massachusetts to find thousands of *unclaimed* acres, and so they came. When they arrived, they found that unclaimed was a relative term. Clear title required that they employ sharp practice, and defend ownership in courts and on the ground, with words, documents, fists, and guns.

The formal process for granting land was relatively simple: the general court in Boston gave proprietors the whole of a specified land mass with the right to keep and develop it, or divide it into building lots to sell or lease. In exchange they were to attract settlers and establish order. To do so, the proprietors set aside land for a church lot, a minister's lot, a school lot, and a government or town hall lot. They built roads, a church, and a town hall. They assured that within three years, a lot leased or sold to an individual would have on it a decent house and twelve cultivated acres. The proprietors had six years to meet these obligations. This was a straightforward process, but there were at least two problems: all those Indians who seemed to think they had a prior claim, and their location at the western edge of New England.

Sheffield—home to Daniel Higby, his sons, and his daughter Lavinia—was the first village settled. The second, in 1739, was just to the north; they called it Stockbridge.

On March 25, 1736, "the General Court granted a township to the Housatonnucks that was six square miles (23,040 acres)."[10] Three years later, a survey laid out thirty-two "interval lots"[11] along the river for the Indians. A sweeping view of the village street made clear that it was a plain along a wide river with gently sloped mountains encircling it. Appropriately called Plain Street, it was the main street in Stockbridge.

In the beginning all the names of title holders on the main street in Stockbridge were Indian names: Mmuhtauwams, Tusnuck, Yokun, and Konaput. That was still true in the 1750 survey. The exception was Thomas Sherman, a white man married to an Indian woman.[12]

Sherman's wife was Yonaka Naunaunocknuck, a Stockbridge Indian. On October 6, 1766, it was voted at town meeting that "whereas Thomas Sherman has, for many year passed, entirely left the town of Stockbridge and left his wife and children helpless and needy that the lands lying in

Stockbridge claimed and possessed by the said Thomas be appropriated to the life and benefit of his said wife and children notwithstanding any disposition said Thomas has or shall make of the same."[13]

Among the first settlers of this New England village was a man who deserted his wife and left his family destitute. Unfortunately that was not unusual in any village in New England. What was unusual was how the town reacted. Granting the woman land may have been just, may have been necessary for the family's survival, may even have been seen as the title reverting to an Indian as originally intended, but it was not commonplace. To grant land to a married woman was not even strictly legal.[14] It may seem compensation for desertion, but desertion was not even accepted grounds for divorce in Massachusetts, nor was it grounds for granting "separate bed and board"—a legal separation with support for the wife.[15] Furthermore, they had the option to warn out Yonaka and her children. They did not. It was unusual, therefore, that the town voted as it did.

In addition to the thirty-two low-lying lots, six "English" received land grants: John Sergeant, Timothy and Joseph Woodbridge (brothers), Ephraim Williams, Ephraim Brown, and Josiah Jones. The English lots were larger but farther up the hill and farther from Plain Street. The riverfront interval or meadow lots were considered the most desirable. "The English were not content."[16]

There was a wresting of the land from the Indians done by "daring and unprincipled men."[17] The first encroachment of white men onto Indian land happened almost immediately in 1739. The white land grantees purchased, leased,[18] or took what they wanted. The general court in Boston, which originally granted the land to the Indians, acquiesced in taking it away. Ephraim Williams may have been the best land grabber, but the Brown brothers, ostensibly retailers, rivaled Williams.

Soon the inhabitants of the street called Plain Street were all white. Is it better that it was done by chicanery rather than violence, by a constant and unkind pressure to be gone?

What is the distance between good business and sharp practice? What Stockbridge would become was formed by the business practices of the men on the hill, not by the idealism of the missionaries, or the goodwill of the Indians on the plain. "The Stockbridge of today, swept clean of its original owners, the Indians, is the actuality that the Williams and the English families up on the hill have built for us."[19]

When Ephraim Williams negotiated the swap of land with the Indians and gave 290 acres "in town" in exchange for 4,000 undeveloped acres, was that good business or sharp practice? When he understood the enormity of the excess value of undeveloped land and knew the Indians did not, was that good business or sharp practice or both? When the Indians were so delighted with the trade that they gave a gift of additional land; when "the English" accepted the gift, was that just good business? When finally the Indians were forced off even that smaller piece of land, and when the government supported the land bandits, what do you call that?

So Main Street Stockbridge at the end of the eighteenth century was no longer a mission. No longer were there Indians and whites living together—Indians on the plain; whites on the hill. No longer was the main street of Stockbridge lined with bark wigwams. It was robbery but not armed robbery, and the Indians, a people dispossessed, quietly left town. The second problem to getting and retaining title to land was a function of location.

On Plain Street, Stockbridge, in this New England White Village,[20] Elizabeth Freeman (Mum Bett) lived across from Esther Edwards's house, where at this time Mrs. Asa Bement was recovering from the winter flu. That house was just a step from Mary Bidwell, who lived catercorner to the Widow Bingham's tavern. These women's lives were controlled not just by the exigency of their roles as women but also by the necessities of creating every institution from the ground up, satisfying the twin social imperatives of unity and order, or suffering the consequences of warning out.

From the Ground Up

Berkshire was (and is) a rectangle nineteen miles wide and fifty miles long. Then as now, it touched New York along its western border, Connecticut on the south, and Vermont at its northern edge. It is far removed from Boston to the east. Isolated from the seat of government, Boston seemed unsure where Berkshire was and possibly uninterested. The result was that the position of the New York–Massachusetts border was an unresolved issue. New York asserted a prior claim to the land being granted by the General Court in Massachusetts.

In 1724, in exchange for 460 pounds, three barrels of cider, and thirty quarts of rum, the Indians sold Berkshire to Massachusetts. Apparently, and unfortunately, in 1705, in lieu of debt, the Indians turned over the same land to New York in a document called the Westenhook Patent. Those trying to settle the Upper and Lower Township of Sheffield were "much impeded, molested, and hindered" by lawsuits, arrests for trespass, and physical attacks by New Yorkers claiming prior ownership. The dispute with New York would be settled but it would take decades to resolve. In 1773, the General Court was again petitioned: land had been partitioned and business transacted but "defects have but recently been discovered, and difficulties might arise. . . . We beg the court to provide a remedy." Once more it was that pesky New York border. After the Revolutionary War, finally, both state governments agreed on a border; it was 1784 before villagers could state with certainty whether they lived in Massachusetts or New York.

There were also internal problems with incorporating, fresh ways for people to gain and lose title to land in a pen stroke. As early as 1726, there was a move to establish a North or Upper Parish, separate from Sheffield, and call it Great Barrington. The proprietors had six years—until 1732—to meet their obligations in exchange for the right to incorporate separately. The strict timeline was neither met in Berkshire nor noted in Boston. Finally in 1743, someone took note and it was discovered that some proprietors had died, others had not fulfilled their obligations, and still others had committed fraud without judicial note.

One duly appointed clerk was David Ingersoll. When the problem was noted, Ingersoll did his job with care and diligence. He divided the land (for the second time) and made careful note of all property lines, owners, and titles. Unfortunately some original proprietors were not granted land; with a flick of Ingersoll's pen they were landless. Naturally they complained. Ingersoll hid the book in which the information was recorded and would not give it up. Finally in 1749, a new clerk was appointed. Timothy Woodbridge was instructed to annul and set aside the land divisions and start anew. He was also instructed to "wait upon Ingersoll" and get hold of the records "by law or otherwise."

Woodbridge wrested the books from Ingersoll and discovered Ingersoll had granted himself major landholdings—the very tracts other proprietors had lost. Due to fraud the land-granting process had to be set aside—again! The great shuffle began: As if North Parish land were a deck of cards, the lots were re-dealt. Proprietors did not end up with the same plots but retained a land mass with the same value; therefore, the new grants were called "equivalents."

After three false starts, in1761 the population of North Parish had grown. Landowners knew what they owned. They petitioned the General Court in Boston so that the North Parish of Sheffield could be set off as a separate village (called a corporation):

> *To His Excellency Francis Bernard, General and Chief over His Majesty's Province of Massachusetts, The Body of the inhabitants of the North Parish of Sheffield are remotely settled from the South Parish in Sheffield, for this and diverse other inconveniences attending, [we request] North Parish be made into a town.*

The request was granted June 30, 1761. North Parish was declared a town with all the privileges enjoyed by other towns. They could establish a Select Board to govern and a town meeting to establish the will of the people that informed the actions of the selectmen. It was pure democracy. However, this newly minted North Parish was denied two common privileges. First the new town was not allowed to send its own representative to the General Court, and could only name a representative jointly with Sheffield. Furthermore the new town had no name. The request made in 1761 did not suggest a name, and no one is certain who ultimately named the town.

The common assumption is that the town was named after Lord Barrington, whose brother Samuel Shute served as Governor of Massachusetts from 1716 to 1723. It seems plausible and a good choice as many towns in the New World sought support from the Old World by selecting names of wealthy and sympathetic members of the peerage. However, that does not answer the question: Why was it named *Great* Barrington? Again, historians are not sure but suggest it had to do with those pesky boundaries between states. There was sufficient confusion for some to suppose that Barrington, Rhode Island, was actually Barrington, Massachusetts. Therefore, the new town distinguished itself by adding the *Great*.

At the first town meeting approximately 500 citizens, including forty-nine freeholders, named town officials, including three selectmen, a treasurer, and a constable. Other officials were named to positions that no longer exist: the Sealer of Leather was an inspector who certified weights and measures; the Hog Reeve was an enforcer of town regulations; a Deer Reeve apprehended those who killed deer out of season; the Fence Viewer inspected property and property lines; the Tithing men collected money due the church; and the Sabbath Wardens reported those who did not attend church on Sunday.

Also on the agenda at the first town meeting was a vote to build a schoolhouse, but it was specified "that there be one and but one schoolhouse at the charge and for the use of the town." The school would be 1,100 square feet, two stories, and have three glass windows.

Money voted to support the town's obligations included no more than 25 pounds for the school building; 35 pounds for the minister, with 10 pounds for his upkeep and that of the church; and 15 pounds for use by the town for roads and other obligations (20 pounds then is approximately $1,400 today; 25 = $1,750; 35 = $2,450; 10 = $700; 15 = $1,050).

It seemed Great Barrington was following in the steps of earlier Berkshire towns and getting organized, but as with the division of land, there were problems. Although they had voted to build a school and did so, at the 1763 town meeting they refused to pay the school builders. It was the year of refusals. The people also refused to "defray the necessary charges of the town" and to "reckon with the town treasurer." In 1764, Great Barrington was cited by the General Court for "not providing a schoolmaster according to law." In 1766, the General Court fined Great Barrington for not keeping its roads in good repair. In letters home, travelers complained bitterly about the condition of the roads and the "surliness" of the people. Great Barrington was experiencing a rough beginning.

On the other hand, Pittsfield moved forward in an orderly fashion, seemingly, according to the book.

In the year 1752, the first settlers arrived. Solomon Deming came from Connecticut with his family. Nathaniel and Judith Fairfield and Charles Goodrich followed shortly thereafter. What they found upon arrival was a vast and beautiful wilderness empty of white settlers. While Sheffield and Stockbridge were incorporated and the Upper Township (Great Barrington) was settled, as Goodrich and Deming moved north, they had to hack their way through woods to arrive on a wild plateau that would, one day, be a city.

Goodrich, Deming, and five other men began immediately to settle the area. In September 1752, they applied to the General Court in Boston to name them the "The Proprietors of the settling lots in the township of Poontoosack." Proprietors, named by the General Court, were entitled to establish the official division of saleable land called the partitions.

In 1753 the General Court granted the application. The proprietors had not been idle. Almost immediately, they identified sixty privately owned lots. In addition, the proprietors set aside "land for the common good"—the minister's lot, ministry lot (for the church), the commons (for the town hall), and the school lot.

The first order of business at the first proprietors' meeting in Poontoosack in 1753 was to "procure some suitable person or persons to preach among us." The second was to erect a church. Third was to "chuse" tax assessors (Deacon Stephen Crofut, Hezekiah Jones, and Jacob Ensign were named), a tax collector (Samuel Taylor II), and treasurer (Charles Goodrich). Goodrich taxed each lot 3 shillings. This sum (3 shillings x 60 lots) was to be the compensation for the minister. In addition Goodrich sought to raise separately 40 pounds to erect the church, and 15 pounds for "the making of roads and bridges." These were the essential organizational steps required for incorporation as a town by the General Court.

There was another requirement for incorporation: population. From 1752 to 1761, the population of Poontoosuck grew from 5 to over 400. With remarkable speed and efficiency, the settlers of Poontoosuck had met the criteria to petition the General Court to become an incorporated town. In 1761, just eight years after Deming and Goodrich set foot on empty wild land, the township of Pittsfield was incorporated. In the same year, virtually at the same moment, the General Court was petitioned to name the westernmost part of Hampshire County a separate county called Berkshire.

Goodrich sat on the committee "to manage the whole affair of the meeting house (church)." Additionally there was a committee to develop the school lot, build roads and bridges, and mark out "a suitable place for the burying of the dead." Finally Charles Goodrich and Deacon Crofut were appointed to seek out and bring to Pittsfield their first preacher.

The man selected, Thomas Allen, served as their minister for forty-six years, and the record shows he was successful in both spiritual and material matters. He left a respectable estate and "Under the ministry of Rev. Thomas Allen 341 members were added to the church; 710 baptisms and 405 marriages were performed."

By 1761, the population of the westernmost part of Hampshire County had grown from negligible to almost 3,000 in five settled communities. Notwithstanding the letter to his brother-in-law, William Williams must have been more relaxed about encouraging people to move to Pittsfield. Now the problem was creating unity and order.

Ideal and Reality: Unity and Order

It is easier to understand excommunicating the argumentative wife in Sheffield, censoring surly residents at the Great Barrington town meeting, ousting a minister whose sermons were out of harmony with common belief, easier to understand the Reverend Allen's meetings of reconciliation, when the ideal of unity and order is understood. The standard was harmony; the aspiration was peace; and the ultimate goal was to regulate and superimpose civilization upon the wild landscape. There was a "standing rule" in the Stockbridge Congregational Church:

> that whenever there appears to be any considerable disagreement
> of opinion in the minds of the brethren ... that meeting shall be
> adjourned in order to give opportunity that they may come to be of
> one mind and act with that unison and harmony which becomes the
> Church of Christ.[21]

Peace, love, and unanimity were the foundations of a Christian life. The relationship was more important than an individual opinion on any matter; it was better to be neighborly than to be right. The effect upon a woman's life was simple to extrapolate: she was unchristian as well as unwanted when she was argumentative or opinionated. She was notable when she was a helpmate, agreeable, and passive. Female babies were given names like "Submit," "Devotion," and "Temperance" as hints to success in future life.

In theory unity and order were by-products of a tame and civilized majority. In practice there were other contributing factors. Those were oligarchy and nepotism.

A survey of the names of judges, selectmen, and representatives to General Court in Boston reveals the same names over and over in any village and the same family names from north to south in Berkshire. It was a clear oligarchy with all power shared among a small defined group of individuals.

It is not hard to understand when you remember the battle between the Constitutionalists and the anti-Constitutionalists. Until the Revolution, it was believed that civil liberty was maintained only by subjection to authority, and that power and authority were divinely ordained. Those few chosen by God served over and over, rotating from judge to deacon, selectman to representative.

Their names were Ashley, Dwight, Partridge, Porter, Pynchon, Stoddard, Williams. They came from Connecticut, where they were called "river gods" or alternately "mansion people." They were inhabitants of the Connecticut River Valley, wealthy and powerful in the church and secular government for generations.

They valued blood relations and group cohesion. Blood and family loyalty were the foundation of control of Berkshire County and other parts of New England. They were believers in dynasty. The names of governors, judges, ministers, and state representatives all over New England were the same as the names of the descendants of Solomon Stoddard.

The Reverend Solomon Stoddard, of Northampton, married Elizabeth Mather, the widow of the Reverend Eleazer Mather, whose pulpit he assumed. With two wives, he fathered eight children. One daughter married the Reverend Timothy Edwards and so Solomon was the grand-father of Reverend Jonathan Edwards. Another daughter married Reverend William Williams, brother of Ephraim Williams Sr., who was the great uncle of Mary Gray Bidwell. Reverend Timothy Edwards was the father of Reverend Jonathan Edwards, whose daughter Esther married Reverend Aaron Burr (Esther and Aaron were the parents of Vice President Aaron Burr). Barnabas Bidwell's sister Jemima married William Partridge, brother of Dr. Oliver Partridge of Stockbridge, whose sister married Dr. Erastus Sergeant. Their sister Sophia Partridge married Elijah Williams, youngest son of Ephraim Williams Sr. [22]

By judicious marriage and careful education of the children, the river gods led in the church and secular communities. They saw themselves as leaders. By their manners and lifestyle they set the tone for refined living. They built large houses, hence the name "mansion people." Elaborate architectural details identified their houses and proclaimed their status: double doors with stone surrounds and the broken-scroll pediment above the door. The river gods were farmers. The land, the thing they understood, was the source of their wealth.

The Williams family controlled Berkshire County from north to south. They handed the baton from father to son, uncle to nephew. When Madam Stoddard sold the land and handed the power to settle Pittsfield to William Williams, she was handing off to a family member.

The Williamses emigrated from England to Massachusetts, and continued to move inland to Hatfield, Stockbridge, and Deerfield, Massachusetts, and Wethersfield, Connecticut. The family connection was strong and carefully maintained. Grafts from fruit trees in Connecticut improved the orchards in Deerfield. Agricultural innovations in Deerfield—such as using manure to fertilize and cradling grain—created surplus that was marketed throughout New England. Their river, the Connecticut, was used to transport the marketable crops.

Their lust for land never abated. The sharp practice that dispossessed the Indians was never regretted. The increase in wealth of one family member was shared, and wealth was the basis, the rationale, for their divine right to power and control. It was a European model—anchored in king and country—soon to be challenged by American upstarts.

In the meantime, they established a hierarchy and sought unity—even if that meant unifying power in their own family's hands—and order—even when that meant that the cantankerous, the rowdy, the dishonest, and those unable to sustain themselves—whether stranger, friend, minister, man, or woman—were excommunicated from the church and warned out of the village.

In the quest for harmony there was dissonance. Schoolmasters and ministers who challenged the power structure were dealt with harshly; ownership was consolidated even when it displaced others, and the poor were ousted rather than succored.

Warning Out

We are content to live among strangers; they were not. Perhaps with a population of 300 million, we have no choice. On the same continent, 250 years ago, there were approximately 3 million inhabitants; 1.5 million in the Colonies. Boston was considered a roiling population center with 17,000.[23] Even as the nineteenth century drew closer, the population grew to just 5 million, and only 6 percent lived in cities.

When Dr. Stephen West came to the pulpit of the First Congregational Church of Stockbridge, there were eighteen English and forty-two Indian families. Indian families tended to have fewer children, and English families more, so a fair estimate of the English population would be (18 x 7 =) 126 and of the Indian population (42 x 3 =) 126, or approximately 252 people.

In a population so small, strangers were rare and stood out. There were church rules and village bylaws that governed dealing with strangers, for gathering them in and for ejecting them. There were religious imperatives and civil regulations for neighborliness and for shunning. Therefore there were clear definitions of strangers. "All who appear openly to reject the laws of Christ we are abundantly taught, in the word of God, to consider as strangers."[24] Simply put, a stranger was an enemy of Christ and therefore not to be taken into the church.

The manner in which an outsider was accepted or rejected in the village was as rigorously observed as was the manner in which a potential congregant was welcomed to communion or excommunicated.[25] First you could not come to a town or village with the intent of abiding there without first obtaining permission. In Pittsfield, and presumably many other New England towns, permission rested upon financial stability.

There were laws designed to prevent vagabond or itinerant pauperism from entering the New England towns and villages. It was called "warning out." In some towns all those "not possessed of a freehold"[26] were warned out. In Pittsfield a vote was taken at town meeting to "warn out in general all those who come into town."[27] The other goal in warning out was to establish unity.

"Berkshire growth rate remained among the highest in the state."[28] In the five years between 1765 and 1770, the population of Stockbridge rose from approximately 217 to 752. In addition, while Williams's letter may seem hyperbolic, in fact, infant mortality dropped. This was a population boom and it had to be controlled.

> *To the Constable of the town of Pittsfield, Greetings, It being reported to us that Nathan Philips and Timothy Thompson and Ichabod Ellithorpe with their families have lately moved into this town and there is danger that they may become burdensome, and expensive to this town. You are therefore thereby required upon receipt of this to notify and warn the said Nathan Philips and Timothy Thompson and Ichabod Ellithorpe that they with their families are directed forthwith to depart from this town under the pain and penalties of the law in such cases made and provided and this shall be your warrant therefore and of your proceedings herein you are to make return to some one of us as soon as maybe. Given under our hands at Pittsfield this first day of April A.D. 1782 Woodbridge Little, James Colt, Matthew Barber, Stephen Crofoot, Selectmen.*[29]

In these three cases the families were really made to leave. There were no social service agencies.[30] The indigent became the obligation of the citizenry. Help was offered from individual to individual. Citizens, who voted to aid a neighboring family, took the coins out of their pockets, the bread from their tables, and the grain from their fields in order to help another. The town as a body and the individuals therein had an obligation to one another unless the needy had been warned out. To protect the village, those who could not support themselves had to leave.

In other cases "warning out" was precautionary. In 1793, for example, Stockbridge warned out everyone who had moved into the village in the last year and threw in the names of a few prominent citizens for good measure.[31] Whether the villagers meant to physically eject someone or meant only to write and sign the warning out document, the reason was the same: They meant to evict all those who could become a financial burden to the town. The blanket "warning out" indicated that while they could stay, henceforth the village was not responsible for their needs.

Since it was rarely money given to the poor for support but more often goods and foods, women, the producers of food and clothing, had the larger role and greatest burden in providing for, and relieving the suffering of, the poor. Furthermore, absent a doctor, the women were expected to nurse the sick. Paradoxically a disproportionately high number of those warned out were women. They were spinsters, widows, or deserted wives who had no means of support, and very often they had children.

Martha and Mary St. John

On the subject of Martha St. John we pass in silence.[32]

The St. John family came to Stockbridge in 1769. Mark and Anna and their seven children—Steven, Mary, Samuel, Ann, Justin, John, and Elijah—were accepted into the village.[33] They were welcomed as members of the Congregational Church "by letter." That meant they were Congregational Church members elsewhere (in this case in Sharon, Connecticut) and brought a letter from their former church attesting that they were members in good standing.

Two years after their arrival, in 1771, the father, Mark, died. Shortly after his death, Anna gave birth to an eighth child, Sarah. Anna was left a widow with eight children and a meager inheritance.[34]

The following year, 1773, daughter Mary was brought before the court.

*Mary Saint John of Stockbridge in said County a single woman
comes here and confesses that sometime on the month of July Anno
Domini 1772 she committed the crime of fornication within the body
of this County. Wherefore it is considered by the Court that now here
she pays at a time to be disposed of according to the law the sum of
thirteen shillings four pence and to pay costs taxed at eight shillings
standing committed until this is performed.*[35]

Mary was fourteen years old and pregnant. "Standing committed until this was performed" meant Mary would be jailed until she could pay the fine and court costs. The father was not named and did not come forward. Anna was unable to pay her daughter's fine, and there was little likelihood of Mary being able to pay and certainly not while in jail.

The fortunes of the family went steadily downhill. In 1772 a daughter Martha was born to Mary. Anna moved with her children and grandchild from Stockbridge to Lenox, Massachusetts, but there was no improvement in their circumstances.

In the town record of Lenox, annual provision is made for the widow. In 1787, however, Anna and four of her children were warned out of Lenox. Mary apparently married, but did not take her daughter Martha into the home of her husband. One son and granddaughter Martha remained behind. They were not warned out because they were employable.

Anna and her four children returned to her people in Sharon. The boy joined the army, and that left Martha St. John.

For a single white female in eighteenth-century Berkshire, a possible road to slavery was fornication.

If a single woman was brought to answer a charge of fornication, she was either pregnant or had just delivered a child. The pregnancy or birth was proof of the act. She was found guilty and fined between 13 and 20 shillings, plus court costs. A shilling in 1800 was about 40 cents or about $2 today, so for between $26 and $40 you could buy a single white female. Here's how.

If the condemned woman could not pay the fine, she was compelled to "stand committed till that sentence be performed."[36] Stand committed meant jailed. At the Lenox town meeting in 1787, it was "voted that the arrearages due from Mr. Elijah Gates on his taxes for the year 1787 be discounted for his keeping Martha St. John."[37]

Gates was being reimbursed the cost of St. John's room and board by a reduction in his taxes. Gates was the constable in Lenox, and he was keeping St. John in his household because she was sentenced to jail and there was, as yet, no jail in Lenox.

Since the woman was unlikely to be able to raise the money to pay the fine while sitting in jail, in order for the court to get its money, anyone could come forward and pay her fine. Therefore in 1787, it was "voted that Martha St. John be put up at Publick Vendue [public sale] and sold to the person who bids her off [buys her]."[38]

By virtue of that payment, St. John was bonded to the purchaser until she repaid the debt. If she could not pay it off, she could work it off.

"Said Martha was setup and bid off [purchased] by Azariah Egleston Esq."

Unfortunately the one who bought her also determined when she was paid in full. Unless she found a protector, a husband, or an avenue back to court for an independent determination, her owner might decide repayment was equal to working the rest of her life.

Even after slavery had been abolished in Massachusetts, the practice of "setting up and bidding off" a woman at "publick vendue" was considered fair and reasonable. The same year that Martha was sold, the man who liberated Mum Bett from slavery, Theodore Sedgwick, sat on a committee with the man who purchased Martha. Together Sedgwick and Egleston were honored with the task of selecting the site, materials, and design for two proposed public buildings—the courthouse and jail.

The following April (1788), the issue of Martha St. John was once again placed before the town meeting. They were asked for advice respecting Martha St. John. The response recorded was: "We pass in silence." It was the equivalent of tabling the item.

It was not until the town meeting of May 1796 that there was a final resolution in the case of Martha St. John. "Voted that the Selectmen be directed to convey as speedily as possible Christian Crow and Martha St. John, two of the state's poor, now residing in this town from hence to the town of Boston and to deliver them to the overseer of the Alms House."[39]

Having dispensed and dispatched Martha, the voters turned their attention to other matters. In a village they must appoint a Sealer of Leather and a Sealer of Weights and Measurers, a Pond Keeper and a Key Keeper, a Fence Viewer and a Sweeper of the Meetinghouse and Streets. This last official placed a matter before the town, to wit: pigs.

Should they allow the pigs loose in the street? Curious: In the records it stated that livestock must be penned. If a ewe, for example, were loose in the street, she could become the property of the one who caught and corralled her. And yet every September at the town meeting the question arose and every September the pigs were let loose. Why? Did it not add to filth and confusion on the byways? Actually it was done to clean the streets. The streets were lined with Chestnut trees. The chestnuts fell; the pigs were let loose and ate the thousands of fallen chestnuts. Wise and thrifty New Englanders saved on feed and spared their backs. The Sweeper of Streets voted in the affirmative.

An Eighteenth-Century Streetscape

At the end of the eighteenth century Stockbridge was no longer a mission. No longer was the main street lined with birch wigwams; no longer were there Indians and whites living together. The Indians were gone from the plain. The English were on the hill, and now on Plain Street English timber-style houses were interspersed with a stage coach inn, dry goods stores, a church, one fortified house, and taverns. It was an "English" (white) village.

An unexpected advantage of the "warning out" issued in 1793 was that it included the occupations of 170 Stockbridge residents. While that was not the total population, it is an interesting cross section, and an indication of whom they considered vulnerable. There were twenty-three spinsters and thirty-one widows; every unwed female was considered economically vulnerable. There were twenty-one Negroes; every nonwhite was considered vulnerable. There were sixteen yeomen (independent farmers), thirty-seven laborers, five joiners, one printer, nine cordwainers (shoemakers), four blacksmiths, one weaver, one clockmaker, three millers, one stone cutter, two schoolmasters, one distiller, one tin man, two carpenters, one tailor, one physician, one Esq. (gentleman), one cooper (maker of barrels), one nailer (maker of nails), one seamstress, two attorneys, one apothecary, one innkeeper, and one saddler.

For all the claims to religious observance, a New England village generally had more taverns than churches. Stockbridge was no exception. There was one church, the Congregational Church, and in the year 1781 there were six holders of innkeeper (taverner) licenses and four retailers of spirits.

There was no concept of zoning; there was only the convenience of mixed use. The stage coach brought mail and news from beyond the hills at first once a week and then more often. The minutes of the 1763 town meeting wherein Williams explained how he took what he wanted from the Indians were posted on a special tree on Plain Street or in the taverns. The citizens of Stockbridge nodded their heads as they read.

The change from Indian Town to New England White Village was quiet without great drama and without bloodshed. It was robbery, but not armed robbery. A people dispossessed quietly move away.

———

Snapshot: It is raining in Stockbridge. In sorrow, a man sits writing a poem to the portrait of his dead wife.[40] He is a lawyer and politician. His house is on the corner of Plain and "the three-rod road" where once Muutauwwams had his wigwam. His law office is a small building behind his house.

Out his window he can look directly down the two-rod road south to hardscrabble Great Barrington and the older, more sophisticated Sheffield. He can probably see the new house and store of the man from whom he purchased his house—Timothy Edwards, prominent citizen, merchant, and son of Reverend Jonathan Edwards.

His name is Barnabas Bidwell, and his wife was Mary Gray Bidwell. Bidwell's house is almost at the center of Plain Street. Called The Elms to honor the tree that stands in front, Bidwell's house is a fine house purchased in anticipation of his marriage. It is the house to which he brought his new wife just fifteen years earlier.[41] Now she is dead.

Just outside his door is the town square. It is made up of three pieces of land sold to the town in 1799 by Josiah Dwight, Barnabas Bidwell, and his mother-in-law, Sarah Spring Gray, for the sum of two dollars.[42]

Barnabas Bidwell
COURTESY OF THE BIDWELL HOUSE MUSEUM, MONTEREY, MASSACHUSETTS

Dwight, owner of a store across the way, is Bidwell's near neighbor living in a house sold to him by Barnabas. Once Plain Street was broken only by the three-rod road, but for two dollars, Stockbridge now has a town square at the mouth of the avenue to the hill.

The hill has a startlingly beautiful prospect. It is the hill the "English" believe has better air, and the hill that forms a curve over the whole plain like sheltering arms. It is where the Williams family lives, and where Jonathan Sergeant lived with his wife Abigail Williams Sergeant. Eventually it will be called Prospect Hill Road.

Plain Street is 132 feet wide. When it rains, as it is doing now, the street is too dirty for ladies such as Mary Bidwell to venture across. When rainy, always conscious of her health, Mary does not even cross the street from her house to visit "the coral house"—home of her cousins the Sedgwicks.

Just down the road is the former home of Jonathan Edwards. He was *the* Jonathan Edwards, minister, scholar, author and originator of the Great Awakening, the intended revitalization of the Congregational Church that caused John Fisk such grief in Stockbridge and the Reverend Hopkins such headaches in Great Barrington.

His daughter Esther Edwards Burr was married from that house on Plain Street. She was younger when she died than Mary Gray Bidwell was when she married. Had Jonathan and Esther lived, she and Mary certainly would have been cordial neighbors and possibly warm friends.

Catercornered on the two-rod road south is the Widow Bingham's "large white house." It is on the corner of Plain Street and the road south (Red Lion Inn today). Retailer Silas Pepoon will later buy the inn from Bingham, and run it into bankruptcy.

Across the three-rod road (Pine Street) is the inn and tavern of Isaac Marsh. In that place John Deane, Revolutionary War soldier and Stockbridge farmer, has his last drink before he dies. To that place, the Widow Deane, still a pleasant woman in good standing, walks to pay his tab. It is before she meets John Fisk, is excommunicated, and leaves town. In fact none of the people bustling along Plain Street see the future.

Bidwell is no more prescient than others. He is surrounded by enemies who will eventually force him off Plain Street and out of Stockbridge as others did the Widow Deane. At one end of Plain Street is Joseph Woodbridge (Main Street tennis courts today) who will issue the arrest warrant. Across the way is the Sedgwick house. They were cousins by marriage and a constant part of Bidwell's family and social circles until the last bond with the Sedgwicks is cut by the deaths of his wife and his mother-in-law. Here the relationship is murky: political opponents, men who disagreed on basic political principles, but also men whom their women bound together. In the end a member of that household will play a key role in the drama that unfolds.

They go about their business. It is a village of walkers and greeters. Does Bidwell greet those who will destroy his aspirations to the Supreme Court as he makes his way along Plain Street? Perhaps, but that is a story for another day.

Between the houses and the shops is a "post office" tree where a notice to "respect your teachers" hangs beside an advertisement that a disgruntled husband will not "pay any debts of my wife's contracting after this date" because "she has left my bed and refuses to return to duty."

For now Bidwell has one grief and no anticipation of any other. He sits and writes to his dead wife:

> *The rain patterns on the roof*
> *And from the eves descends.*
> *The storm keeps visitants aloof*
> *And even shuts out friends.*
> *So sweetly all my moments flew*
> *When Mary was my bride*
> *How oft I do those scenes review*
> *With Mary at my side.*[43]

The Taverns

> *I always thought it great prudence and Christianity . . . [to have]*
> *regulation of such houses.*[44]

It began as an agricultural community. The main concern was survival: protection from starvation, the elements, and wild animals, especially wolves. It was isolated and insular, with a population that had scant resources or energy for the amenities. The community had just sixty housing lots. Then it grew, and by the time Pittsfield was incorporated in 1761, it had changed from wilderness to burgeoning community.

Indications of growth in Pittsfield were the rising population, the improvement in the domestic arrangements, and the building of a church, a town hall, forges, mills, and taverns.

A tavern, Newburyport
ALICE MORSE EARLE, *HOME LIFE IN COLONIAL DAYS*, 1898, P. 354

In other parts of Massachusetts, the first taverns had wonderful names: the Tree of Knowledge, Bunch of Grapes, Green Dragon, Orange Tree, and Red Horse. They also had terrible reputations. In 1696, Judge Nathaniel Saltonstall wrote the Salem Court: "I always thought it great prudence and Christianity . . . to state the number of publique houses in towns and [to have] regulation of such houses . . . thereby to prevent all sorts of wickedness which grows daily . . . in these pest houses and places of enticement."

Sixty-five years later, in Pittsfield, the judge had won his point. The colorful names were gone, taverns were known simply by the names of the owners, and licensing of taverns was required. Furthermore, between 1761 and 1762, the taverner license became known as the innkeeper license, perhaps to remove any taint. The word *tavern* was used interchangeably with *inn* and *public house*. The latter was a good descriptor because taverns were often located in converted farm or town houses.

On the other hand, sometimes the words *coffee house* were used and it was hard to imagine why since coffee was rarely served. Early residents bought coffee and drank it at home, but it was not brewed in taverns because, in the opinion of many eighteenth-century folks, brewing coffee produced an "evil smell." The most popular drinks were punch, cider, grog, beer, ale, Madeira, syllabub (sweetened milk or cream curdled with wine) and flip (sweetened beer heated with a rum or brandy mixture added).

Early Pittsfield taverns were not rowdy places; they were regulated as Saltonstall had wished. It was unlawful to dance in a tavern or to play dice, cards, or other gambling games. Pittsfield taverns were established along the main stage coach lines. The streets of Pittsfield were named for the direction in which they pointed: East Street to Boston, West Street to Albany, and South Street to Hartford and Hudson. Those that attracted the business of travelers as well as locals faired best.

The first to receive a taverner license in Pittsfield was Daniel Hubbard in 1762; his tavern was on West Street. Other early taverns were owned by David Noble (on the East side of town), Captain John Strong on East Street, and Captain James Easton (the paramour) on South Street.[45]

Today we would not think of a tavern as part of the cultural life of a town, but in the eighteenth century, it was. In taverns, the population came together, local news was exchanged, clubs were formed, and club meetings were held. Before post offices, mail was received at taverns delivered by the stage coaches, books were collected and exchanged, local newspapers and out-of-town newspapers, delivered with the mail, were read and discussed.

Taverns were also part of eighteenth-century political life. The minutes of the town meeting were posted there as were the eighteenth-century version of legal notices: "Mr. X declares that he will no longer pay the bills of his wife Mrs. X as she is profligate." In the late 1700s, in taverns, a revolution was plotted. Reputedly, John Adams, John Quincy Adams, and Daniel Webster drank at Pittsfield taverns. Taverners David Noble and John Strong were among the first Pittsfield residents to stand for liberty and the Revolution. During the Revolution, when the civil courts were closed, it was at James Easton's Tavern that arbitrations of civil matters were heard.

Women were indeed allowed in taverns and were served there. There is some evidence that at least one woman plotted her life as a spy in a tavern.[46]

Fifty years later, Pittsfield taverns had become a place for celebrations. Thanksgiving and the Fourth of July dinners were eaten in taverns.

Park Square in Pittsfield
JOHN WARNER BARBER, *HISTORICAL COLLECTIONS*, 1841, P. 87

As times changed and the church loosened its grip on mundane matters, music and dancing were added to the larger taverns. Ballrooms were built for dances and parties. The ballrooms were usually on the second floor, and sometimes a second floor had to be built for the purpose.

As the War of 1812 approached, Ingersoll's, Keeler's, and Merrick's Taverns were added on North Street, and Stanton's Tavern on East Street. General Lafayette was fed at a grand dinner on the second floor of Merrick's. Also at Merrick's, a party of Federalists were declined service at the Fourth of July dinner because Merrick was an anti-Federalist. This only caused the Federalists to come together, raise the money, and open their own tavern on Park Square—wherein, they promised, to serve everyone. At Keeler's, a converted farmhouse, there was dancing for the soldiers billeted at Pittsfield.

Taverns were often the place to receive the earliest news from beyond the Berkshire Hills. As the War of 1812 seemed to be drawing to a close, Pittsfield residents gathered at Hubbard's Tavern, and waited anxiously for word of the outcome. Knowing people depended on the line for news from other parts in the country; the stage coach company printed large pieces of paper with black lettering and affixed the papers to each side of the coach. As the stagecoach rolled into Berkshire County all could read the word: "Peace."

Widow Bingham's Tavern

A person of sober life and conversation [who] is suitably qualified & provided for as an inn holder in the town of Stockbridge.[47]

Anna Dix was born in Watertown, Massachusetts, in 1745. At eighteen, she moved with her family to Berkshire County. In1863 her mother died in childbirth and it was customary for her father to assume Anna would now care for her baby sister Lydia.

Anna finds her way into the official record in September 1765 when she is tried for the crime of fornication in the Court of General Sessions. The belly is proof, and the birth proof positive. Anna is convicted and fined. Unlike Mary St. John, Anna pays her fine and on November 14, 1765, marries the minister's son. It is the new minted family of Thomas Orton Jr., his wife Anna Orton, and son James Orton. Was Thomas the father?

The marriage was short-lived. By 1773, if not earlier, Anna is divorced because that year she remarries. Her new husband is Silas Bingham of Great Barrington. She was twenty eight; Silas was forty-one and a successful retailer.

It is worthy of a pause to consider this unexpected life. By twenty-eight years old Anna has defied a number of moral precepts and common laws and is apparently thriving. She was not done with trail blazing.

Two years later Anna and Silas left Great Barrington. They purchased two acres of land in Stockbridge on the corner of Plain Street and the road south from the widow of Abraham Brimsmaid, tailor. On the property were a house, a barn, and a tailor shop. Anna and Silas opened a store.

In 1775 Stockbridge had a population of 1,200 divided, according to some, into 1,000 white settlers and 200 Mahican Indians, and to others, 900 white settlers and 300 Mahican Indians. By comparison, in 1772, the population of Pittsfield was 138 families.

Isaac Brown, Joseph Woodbridge, and Timothy Edwards became licensed retailers in 1757, 1762, and 1772, respectively. In 1773 William Goodrich petitioned and received a license "for keeping a house of publick entertainment." Therefore, in addition to the Bingham store, there may have been as many as three other retailers, and an inn in Stockbridge.

Since Plain Street was a North-South connector road, there were stage coaches as well as Revolutionary War troops moving through the village. It was a New England crossroads; even Ethan Allen traveled Plain Street and stopped at Bingham's store.[48] He purchased a jackknife on his way to the Battle of Ticonderoga. Indeed, in the eighteenth century, Stockbridge could have been described as bustling.

The Binghams met the need and expanded their business to an inn and tavern. All went well until January 6, 1781, when Silas Bingham died at the age of forty-nine. Anna continued to operate the inn and tavern as usual.

> *The jurors for the Commonwealth of Massachusetts for the body of the said county do on their oath present that Anna Bingham of Stock-bridge in the County of Berkshire widow at said Stockbridge on the fifteenth day of September last past and from that time until the first day of January current did wickedly and unlawfully and with force and arms presume to be a common victualler, innholder taverner and seller of wine beer and strong liquor without being duly licensed.*[49]

If Anna was to continue to operate, she needed a license. The license cost 20 pounds, and required people to stand surety, that is, vouch for the applicant and promise to pay the fee should the licensee be unable. Moreover, in Berkshire County, no such license had ever been issued to a woman.

Two important men of Stockbridge, Theodore Sedgwick and William Goodrich, stood surety, promising 10 pounds each, and certifying that Anna was "a person of sober life and conversation, suitably qualified ... for an inn-holder in the town of Stockbridge." The names Sedgwick and Goodrich may have lent weight to her petition; in addition Anna wrote a letter. In this case, the spelling, capitalization, and punctuation are unchanged because they are an indication of both the breadth and limitations of an otherwise competent eighteenth-century woman.

> *Your petitioners late Consort Mr. Bingham of Stockbridge dyed the last winter. for Some years before his Death he had made tavern keeping his whole Business, that for his Accommodation And that*

87

of travelers he had laid out great part of his Estate in A large and Elegant house. Your petitioner was therefore left without any other means to obtain A livelihood for herself and Fatherless children but tavernkeeping.[50]

In short, Anna, petitioner and widow of Mr. Bingham, was left with a house and no other means of support. Silas spent a considerable part of his fortune either enlarging the house on the property or building a new one. In either case, the result was a large elegant house, and a bankrupt estate.

Anna went on to explain that in Berkshire County, since the courts were closed by the Constitutionalists during the period, she was unsure or unable to do what was necessary.

The letter demonstrated that Anna was literate, and also, persuasive. Passing over the fact that the courts reopened and her husband died in the same year, 1781, Anna Bingham's letter was successful. In 1781 Anna became the first female victualler, inn-holder, taverner, and seller of wine liquor and strong liquor in Berkshire County.

Three years later, Anna was again dogged by governmental requirements. This time it was taxes.

I am not insensible that the time has lapsed for payment of my excise, but I am under the disagreeable necessity to inform you that it is incompatible with my business to attend to Great Barrington.[51]

Like Joseph traveling to Bethlehem, Anna was required to pay her taxes in a town a few miles away. She did not choose to close her business in order to make the trip. In jest or exasperation or merely high hope, she asks the tax collector to come to Stockbridge.

You must be sensible of my peculiar circumstances and also of the curse which attends those who devour widows' houses . . . wish only, Sir, to see you at my house and no doubt I'll satisfy you to your content.[52]

For the next thirteen years, Anna conducted business. She welcomed guests, diners, and merry-makers just as they are welcomed on the same corner today. It was not, however, all beer and skittles. From the time of her husband's death, creditors dogged her steps and regulators and the tax men kept a sharp eye.

In 1794 she was convicted of operating "not having been first duly licensed according to law." Anna did not have 20 pounds for the license renewal in 1793, and attempted, for some months, to operate without one. Anyone operating an inn and tavern without a license was "ordered to pay as a fine the sum of twenty pounds and the costs of prosecution taxed at five pounds eleven shillings and one penny," and if they could not pay, was "committed to Sheriff Satteree until the fine be disposed of."

The next thirteen years brought more legal and economic problems that found the widow repeatedly back in court. If court appearances were granted credits at law schools, by the end of her life, Anna could have received a law degree.

On April 20, 1807, twenty-three investors in the Housatonic River Turnpike met at the "dwelling house of Anna Bingham." Anna held thirty shares, one of the three largest shareholders. The turnpike was to connect West Stockbridge, Stockbridge, Lee, and New Marlborough and there to connect to the through-road from Hartford to Lenox. On June 1, 1807, they met again at the "dwelling house lately owned by Anna Bingham." So we know Anna sold her elegant house between April and June 1807. The purchaser, fellow turnpike shareholder and Stockbridge neighbor Silas Pepoon, was not an experienced taverner or inn-holder, and his debts exceeded even those of the Widow Bingham. He struggled along for five years, but in 1812, his property was seized by creditors. Pepoon was conducted to the jail at Lenox, and Bingham Tavern, later the Red Lion Inn, was sold at auction for $12.

As Anna left Stockbridge, across Plain Street, Mary Bidwell sat writing to Barnabas about his "jaunt to Monticello"; Pamela Sedgwick suffered another attack, the penultimate; she would soon die. Across South Street Timothy Edwards once more wrote his nephew, Aaron Burr, urging a visit expressing his pleasure if he would come. Edwards would have to wait another two years, but eventually the former vice president, formerly accused and acquitted traitor, the duelist and womanizer, would come.

It was a curious village—small and seemingly unimportant, certainly remote, and yet, filled with people of note, and events worth recording. And for many years, it was where an inn and tavern was owned and operated by a woman—the only woman in Berkshire County, and one of a precious few in New England, to obtain a license to do so.

Chapter 5

The Social Circle

My fire is out and low the light
Reluctantly I say goodnight
For soon will dawn the coming day
Adieu, my friend, your Mary Gray.[1]

Pedigree

A woman's social circle was of scant interest to a man, except when it was.

A woman was not an equal or a consultant to her husband, except when she was. Mary Gray Bidwell had the family relations, social connections, education, wit, and charm to make her indispensable to her husband.

Her grandmother was Sarah Williams, the older sister of Ephraim Williams Sr. Sarah married James Gray, a weaver in Hadley, Massachusetts, and together they had two sons, James Jr. and John. In 1749 Mary's grandfather sold his land in Hadley and purchased 200 acres from their nephew Col. Ephraim Williams Jr. at the north end of Stockbridge.[2]

Six years later in 1755, Colonel Williams died during a battle of the French and Indian War. Among the bequests,[3] he left fifty acres to his cousins, James Jr. and John Gray. Through her maternal line, Mary Gray Bidwell was related to the Connecticut river gods, and to those who maintained political control of Western Massachusetts. Intimacy and kinship with the Stoddard, Partridge, and Williams families were of immeasurable use to her husband and political aspirant, Barnabas Bidwell.

Mary's father, James Gray Jr., married Sarah Spring. Sarah was a first cousin of Pamela Dwight, daughter of Abigail Williams Sergeant

Mary Gray Bidwell
COURTESY OF THE BIDWELL HOUSE MUSEUM, MONTEREY, MASSACHUSETTS

Dwight and General Joseph Dwight. Pamela Dwight married Judge Theodore Sedgwick. Through her paternal line, Mary Gray Bidwell brought her husband into a family circle that included the most prominent and politically powerful in Berkshire County. Mary's family ties allowed Barnabas to remain part of a charmed social circle despite sharp political differences.

With that introduction, meet the exceptional Mary Gray Bidwell. Born in 1764, she was ten years old when the Revolutionary War started and eighteen when it ended. She was born in the eighteenth century, but the post–Revolutionary War period belonged to her generation.

In her early life, probably because her father suffered from both illness and severe economic setbacks,[4] Mary was sent to live with her mother's brother, Dr. Marshall Spring in Watertown, Massachusetts. There she received an education not possible in Stockbridge. It may be difficult to think of a New England village as the frontier, but Stockbridge, on the western edge of New England, was.

Marriage

Marriage is the grand lottery of life.[5]

On February 21, 1793, at her uncle's inn Watertown, Mary Gray, twenty-nine years old, and Barnabas Bidwell, thirty-two, were joined in marriage by the Reverend Richard R. Eliot.

Although they were married at the end of the eighteenth century, they enjoyed a thoroughly modern marriage—that is, it was a love match. Not too many years before, a woman married whom she was told to, to avoid the ignominy of spinsterhood and to gain advantage for the family as a whole. A few years hence Mary's neighbor, Catharine Sedgwick, would refuse a suitor, choose to be a spinster, because she did not "love him sufficiently."[6] Of all the changes that would occur in a woman's life post–Revolutionary War, the rights to vote, own property, and work outside the home, the changing basis of marriage, the right of woman to choose was the most important. Without recognition of a woman's value for who she was not just what she could do, without a basis for mutual love and respect between the sexes, without equity in intimacy none of the other was possible, or even contemplated.

There was a significant difference between a married woman addressed as Goodwife or Goody and one addressed as Madam just as there was a significant difference between a literate person and an educated one. In both instances, Mary was the latter.

One year earlier Barnabas purchased a house called The Elms on the corner of Pine and Plain Streets in Stockbridge. Soon after the ceremony Barnabas took Mary to her new home. Mary's household was large and eventually accommodated a large family. From the outset, her mother Sarah Gray lived with them.

Sarah's husband brought her to Stockbridge in 1761. The land left to them by Williams enlarged their homestead and holdings. His family connections secured Gray a position as Commissary General of the United States for the Northern Department during the Revolutionary War. They would have been just fine financially if Gray had not become so ill at so young an age. As it was, Sarah was widowed and destitute in 1782. She lived in straitened circumstances until she entered Mary's house in 1793. Sarah remained in Stockbridge, and for more than forty years was a member of the Congregational Church under the ministry of her friend and cousin by marriage the Reverend Stephen West.[7] The last sixteen years of her life she spent at The Elms.

Mary also welcomed a nephew into her home. She and Barnabas had two children, a son Marshall and daughter Sarah. Marshall was named after her uncle in Watertown, and Sarah after her mother. The daughter was called Sally to differentiate the two Sarahs in the house.

Mary's duties included caring for her mother, educating the three children, meeting her many social obligations for her own enjoyment as well as her husband's advancement, regulating her household, and managing her husband's law office. Barnabas was often away in Boston and Washington, D.C., serving as state senator, US Congressman in the Jefferson administration, and Attorney General of Massachusetts. Their consolation and our window into their lives were their letters.

The Letters

Yours just come has been 12 days in its passage.[8]

Mary's letters were filled with affection, but at times with exasperation at the slowness of the post.

In addition to treating Mary with affection, in the exchange of letters between them, there was a note of deference in Barnabas's tone. Barnabas wrote, "I acknowledge myself always indebted to you . . . I am disposed to be paying and at the same time contracting debts of this kind."[9]

Remarkably Barnabas told Mary about the matters being discussed in the US House of Representatives as well as in the taverns without condescension or censorship. He detailed events not as if her mind were too weak to comprehend but as if he wished her to be fully informed in exchange for her point of view. It was long removed in years and attitude from Governor John Winthrop's opinion, "if she had not gone out of her way and calling to meddle in such things as are proper to men, whose minds are stronger, [she would have] kept her wits."

Nor was Mary coy or shy, but shared her opinion forthrightly. She wrote,

The subject of importing slaves, I observe, is brought up at your board. I am confident you will oppose with your utmost energy this wicked inhuman traffic. Assuredly this is first in the black catalogue of our crimes as a nation, and it must soon draw down the vengeance of an offended righteous God, not only upon the barbarous wretches who barter human flesh, their fellow men!—But upon all who do not bear testimony against this abomination. "Who stoppeth his ears at the cry of the poor, he also shall cry himself, but not be heard." I should not perhaps have written so much upon this subject if I had not known that your sentiments, my dear friend, were perfectly congenial to mine upon this important point.[10]

She praised Barnabas when he followed her advice. "For your animated defense of the poor oppressed Africans, I thank you, and honor you from my heart."[11]

She was also deft at gently chiding her ambitious husband. On January 16, 1806, Mary wrote, "As our election approaches, the annual slanders, calumny and detraction of the Federal presses, are hurried into circulation with a zeal and activity worthy of a better cause. For the honor of the Republican cause, I hope, such weapons will be exclusively Federal." This she wrote to the man, politician, and Republican whom former President Adams described as the user of "dispassionate and deliberate sophistry and misrepresentation."[12]

In the eighteenth century, among the roles of a woman was providing the family its moral compass. On January 16, 1806, Mary wrote Barnabas,

I am astonished at the progress of civilization produced by the benevolent exertions of our government among our savages. Let their enemies (the enemies of the government) revile. It is the only consolation they can enjoy while they possess such bitterness of spirit. If the most generous efforts to increase the sum of human happiness and diminish the evils and woes, which involve our fellow men of whatever nation, will not entitle to applause then Mr. Jefferson cannot deserve it for his exertions in the cause of suffering humanity. But the future generations . . . will do him the justice which some of his contemporaries refuse.

And this:

December 29, 1806 Should a majority of your honorable body thus legalize this oppression [slavery] what a disgrace it would reflect upon the name of Republican but it is a satisfaction to know that you, and yours, are exculpated from the guilt of this atrocious sin.

In whatever manner Barnabas was judged in public, at home he was accurately described as a man who loved and revered his wife and cherished his children. When he was at home in Stockbridge but Mary was away, Barnabas wrote her that he was "homesick." When she was at home and he was away, Mary was both wistful and playful: "You are tenderly remembered tho a democrat."[13]

Education

You know that I as well as your good Mama and Grandmamma always consider you a young gentleman of your word; I depend on your doing as you have informed me you intend to do.[14]

Thus began Barnabas's letter of instruction to his young son Marshall, March 15, 1806. Marshall was an only son so all the hopes and aspirations of the father rested on him.

There was a distinct difference between literacy and education. Literacy could mean as little as signing your name legibly and distinguishing random words on a page. Education came in levels; the highest was reserved for white males of means.

At any level of society, it was the obligation of the mother to teach the children to read and write; if she herself could. Once that minimum was accomplished, the boys were turned over to the father for education and the girls remained with the mother to learn their roles.

Barnabas was in the unenviable position of having to exercise his obligation from a distance. The letter went on:

> *Your kind pretty letter dated February 27 pleased me very much. I am glad to learn from your own letter that you hope to behave as I wish and that you intend to study and learn....You tell me your instructor is an exceedingly good one. To like your instructor is generally a good sign; for good scholars commonly like their masters.... In the meantime I depend on you to conduct like a gentleman, and to do errands and to wait on your Grandmamma and Mama, to do chores and keep things in order in the house and woodhouse and barn ... attend to your studies and improve your manners and behavior.*[15]

It was up to the father to teach a son his proper role in society; this letter is a fair sampling of expectations for a young boy.

January 26, 1806, Mary wrote to Barnabas about their daughter:

> *Sally's genius, if I may use the word, seems so versatile. She may acquire almost any science she attempts. You may recollect, my dear friend, that I explode the idea of mental sexuality ... it is formed by education. Such children certainly deserve a mother of the first knowledge and acquirements or the [possessor] of decent education— if their father is engaged in public life at a distance.*[16]

In the final sentence, gentle Mary delivers a rebuke so slight it barely registers. In addition, she "explodes the idea of mental sexuality"—in short, she believes a woman's intellectual abilities might equal a man's.

Western view of Williams College and other buildings.

Williams College JOHN WARNER BARBER, *HISTORICAL COLLECTIONS*, 1841, P. 105

In New England there was what we would call an elementary school where both boys and girls attended. Colleges and other institutions of higher learning were reserved for the boys. Some New England villages evinced no interest in educating their children. For example, Great Barrington would not approve the expenditure for schoolhouse or teacher. In Stockbridge, there was the will to educate the children; the problem in Stockbridge was lack of teachers.

In Stockbridge on January 26, 1806, Mary continued, "Some of our neighbors, Dr. Pomeroy, Major Brown, etc. seem pleased with my proposal for establishing a winter subscription school if . . . cannot be obtained to employ a capable instructor."[17]

The following year, Mary was concerned about Marshall. "Marshall stands second in the boy's class, Josiah, only above him. Indeed he has once been at the head. Tho' yet he does not love his school."[18]

Mary was certainly "that mother of first knowledge" capable of overseeing their education, but the prejudices or at least the fixed ideas of centuries were not wholly absent in the Bidwell household. Mary's young son perhaps innocently but very clearly expressed the notion of male intellectual superiority.

"Marshall," Mary writes, "with artless tenderness assured me yesterday that he should be very happy to teach me arithmetic."[19]

Entertainments and Celebrations

I congratulate you on the safe arrival of your china, and wish you much comfort in the use of it. Should I live to return, tho not a connoisseur in such things, for your sake I expect to value and enjoy it.[20]

While Mary had tea with Mrs. Edwards and the squire at their house on South Street, and visited regularly the Sedgwicks in the house across Plain Street, she was as often the hostess. On New Year's Eve 1805, she wrote Barnabas: "Yesterday your good brother sent me an excellent pig, I have invited Capt. and Mrs. Whiton, their two oldest daughters, Mr. Blair, Mr. Taylor to tea and sup upon your Brother's present this night."

In celebration of New Year's Day there was a village-wide open house: neighbors walked from house to house exchanging gifts and pleasantries. New Year's Eve was celebrated much as it is now.

Mary goes on, "I am sensible roast pig is not exactly the dish for fashionable supper, but tho not above fashion here, we are independent enough to deviate from its rigid laws whenever we choose." Indeed she was sensible of fashion and etiquette. Vassal White wrote of her:

In polished society she well was regarded:
Her manner mild her taste refined
She social talents always shone
Her wit and charm for every kind[21]

Though she was conversant with the rules of polite society, Mary was also secure enough to take up a rule and break it, or as Teddy Wharton would say a generation later: "Mr. Wharton if I were you I should not do that." "Young man, if I were *you* I could not."

On January 1, 1807, each made a special effort to present the compliments of the season. Mary wrote, Most sincerely and affectionately, do I invoke the richest blessings upon my dear friend, not as the compliment of the season, but as the warmest sentiments of my heart. This benediction I must acknowledge can boast less of benevolence than that ante-deluvian [antiquated] quality—selfishness.[22]

From Barnabas: Permit me, my dearest friend, to present you the compliments of the season. I most cordially wish you a happy New Year. This letter is the first paper, which I have dated in the New Year.

Barnabas took the opportunity to mark the occasion with a depiction of his wife: "But my first attention, on this anniversary, is due to the friend of my heart, the mother of my children, the companion of my life, the participator of my hopes and fears, my joys and sorrows. Accept, my dear Mary, my most affectionate and cordial salutation."[23]

These were special greetings fashioned for a special occasion. If that sounds like a Christmas card or Valentine, there is good reason. For them New Year's Day was the gayest and most joyously celebrated winter holiday. Christmas was serious and ceremonial; Valentine's Day belonged to the next century.

While at home eighteenth-century wives may have been welcoming and frisky according to William Williams, an eighteenth-century Christmas was sober and solemn. The Christmas tree strapped to the top of the family sedan, mothers shopping, children fairly gamboling down the street in anticipation of the goodies in store for them—that is the iconic vision of a New England Christmas. We accept it, and think it was always so, but it was not.

Massachusetts Bay Colony, December 25, 1621: It was a regular work day; those who wished not to work in honor of the holiday were scoffed at. Unimaginable? Well, imagine this: May 11, 1659, celebrating Christmas was outlawed in Massachusetts, and those who dared celebrate Christmas were fined 5 shillings. The law was enacted to put a stop to "disorders arising in several places within the jurisdiction [Massachusetts] by reason of some still observing such festivities."

The disorders were not insignificant. The celebration of choice on Christmas Day was "wassailing," an Old World custom reinvented in the New World. In England, wassailing was like caroling: the poorer members of the community went to the "better" houses and sang in exchange for food and drink. In New England, rather than standing outside the house, they entered the kitchen to receive food and drink.

In Massachusetts wassailing began to resemble "breaking and entering." Wassailers entered the home of one elderly couple known for their good wines and brandies. They sang and demanded "the best." When the couple offered beer but declined to offer pear brandy, violence resulted. The end was conflagration: they burned down the house. The law against Christmas was, at its core, a law against drunkenness, fights, and gaming.

In 1681 the law against Christmas was repealed. For sixty years, citizens of Massachusetts had not celebrated Christmas so the action did not result in immediate change. Even in the early eighteenth century, almanacs did not print *December 25* in red ink—that is, did not indicate it was a "red letter day," a holiday. In 1761, the birthday of Great Barrington, Pittsfield, and Berkshire County, there was a newspaper editorial supporting the celebration of Christmas but warning that it be celebrated as a "most solemn festival [without] disorder or immorality."

Christmas as we know it, the trees and wreaths, bells and caroling, gifts and good food, is a nineteenth-century invention. The authors, literally, of the modern celebration were a Stockbridge spinster and a German immigrant: Catharine Sedgwick and Charles Follen. Follen wrote a story of Christmas, describing it as a holiday for children. His story featured something unknown in America at the time, something that has become the central image of our modern holiday—the Christmas tree.

It was the girl across the street, the one Mary remembered lying prostrate after her mother's death; it was Catharine Sedgwick who drew the indelible picture of rosy-cheeked children, their eyes alight with happiness on Christmas morning in her novels and stories.

Catharine borrowed from her experiences in New York City, where Christmas was celebrated with gifts and a Christmas feast, to create her fictional Christmas. She relied heavily on the celebrations of New Year's Day in Stockbridge: at her home, at the Bidwell house, up and down Plain Street. New Year's Day was the New England holiday that included open house parties, food, presents, and children's games.

Together Follen and Sedgwick transformed the image of Christmas from one of adult carousing into one of innocent joy. In 1856 Christmas was made a legal holiday in Massachusetts.

It was another one hundred years before Norman Rockwell captured the classic images, physical and emotional, that are a New England Christmas. During those one hundred years, all the elements of celebration were gathered from around the world, around the country, and from other New England holidays, and collected into our modern celebration of Christmas: songs from England; the tree from Germany; the jolly gift-giver from Scandinavia, Ireland, and Germany; and recipes from the world over. With them came the joy of giving and the angst about gift selection; feasting and the fear of excessive caloric intake; drinking and the designated driver; and the never-ending commercials. Still, it is a treasured family affair and a vast improvement over the disreputable excess or dreary nothingness of the seventeenth and eighteenth centuries.

The Utility of Society

When Charles Sedgwick, trembling and pale sent up a request that I attend his Mama who was suddenly very ill; I ran for my cloak. . . . With pain I add, that Mrs. Sedgwick's derangement returns with her increasing strength.[24]—*MB to BB, February 28, 1806*

It was not possible in a world turned by manual labor, the world prior to the Industrial Revolution, for any single family unit to survive unaided. Neighbors helped. With manpower and horses from her own household and that of her neighbor's, Mary laid in the wood necessary to heat the house in winter.

"We now have, near forty cord[25] of wood, drawn since I last wrote you. John employed Enoch Humphrey and Park in chopping while he with our horses and Edward H with Captain Whitney's [horses] for six days brought wood as fast as the strength of the animals would permit."[26]

In the social circle, women came together and worked. Quilting and sewing bees multiplied the hands to ease the labor. The woman's circle made clothes and food for the poor, and it was dispensed from their circle. That was how the women were employed in Stockbridge when the irresponsible lad left off loading the cart and took a young girl's ribbon.[27]

Vassal White remembered Mary's largess and wrote:

The tale of suffering or of woe
Was never told to her in vain
Her bounties made the wretched glow
Relieved their wants and eased their pain.[28]

~~~

A neighbor's help was necessary in health and especially in times of illness. Sarah Gray outlived both of her daughters. It was clear indication that life was dangerous; there was scant defense against nature, and illness was too often fatal. Sarah faced widow's weeds, destitution, and the death of a child within a few years. From 1782 to 1788, she buried her husband and then rushed to the side of her oldest daughter, remained with her, nursing her, until she passed away in 1788.[29]

Illness was rampant and doctors were rare. A village with one doctor was indeed rich. Supplementing his efforts or standing in for the doctor was woman's work. Anxiety about one's own health and the health of all family members was ever present. There was nothing casual about the question "How are you?"

"By your letter I find the jaunt to Monticello was far different from a party of pleasure. If however, by tour, by giving a little free country air, benefits your health, I am at least glad."[30] Almost every letter from Mary contains the neighborhood health report, a survey of friends and family.

Stockbridge, January 16, 1806, from Mary: "Doctor Sergeant[31] called upon Mama this evening and seems much encouraged. Her cough has not quite left her."

February, 28, 1806: "Captain Whitney is confined with a bilious fever and I fear dangerously ill. Mrs. Porter is sick with a disorder similar to that which so often distressed Judge John Bacon.[32] Judge Bacon continues low, I am told. We have not seen him since you left home."

March 6, 1806: "I hear that T. Allen [the Reverend Thomas Allen of Pittsfield] is ill at Boston with the fatal epidemic prevalent there."

Stockbridge, March 31, 1806, Mary to her husband: "Again, my dear friend, I write from the chamber of sickness. I hope, however, soon to exchange it for a less gloomy apartment, for gloomy it is, notwithstanding the uniform calm, cheerful submission of the dear invalid [Mary's mother Sarah]."

December 29, 1806: "Capt. Whitney is again very ill. I much apprehend this distressing disease will terminate fatally. Mrs. Bement is recovering. [When the Bement family first arrived in Stockbridge, they lived in the home vacated by the Reverend Jonathan Edwards when he left the Congregational Church of Stockbridge in 1758 to assume the position of President of the College of New Jersey (later Princeton). That was just a few doors down from Mary.] Clark Whitney is yet very low."

Stockbridge, September 21, 1807:

Cato was dispatched after the Judge [Sedgwick] and another messenger for his sons at Albany, a little before eight yesterday morning, and in fifteen minutes after, Mrs. Sedgwick closed a life of uncommon suffering;[33] commencing as we have reason to hope, a happy immortality! When I reflect upon the unmurmuring, and even cheerful submission, [with] which she uniformly exhibited in her lucid hours, under a most distressing personal calamity. When in considering her many virtues, this is added to the number. I feel I must pronounce her, one of the most exalted of her sex. The family is deeply afflicted. Catharine [Sedgwick] fainted yesterday repeatedly. Today, I sent to know if I could be useful, but finding my services were not required, I rode with Sally and Marshall as charioteer since the sun softened the air. Tomorrow morning I am informed my assistance will be acceptable. Mr. Watson has this day been called to Hartford to attend his expiring mother. [Sedgwick son-in-law] And now, my friend, I render you my affectionate thanks for your letter from Northampton. To find you arrived so seasonably was very gratifying. The indisposition you felt, just before you left home, authorizes me to repeat my parting injunction and entreaty, "be cautious of your health" and "employ a physician seasonably." The frequent deaths in our neighborhood seem calculated to enforce the conviction that we too are indeed mortal. How many deaths, my dear friend, have

I loved to announce! Soon may the pen of another record mine! My health indeed, at present, is as good perhaps better, than when you left home. I promised Sally the opposite page, but I shall find a spot for post script tomorrow. I will now say only good night. M. B. What can you say now in vindication of Judge Marshall?[34]

Her Circle

Since she was related to the families that mattered, had a fine visage and the finest manners, Mary socialized with the first circle.

She wrote Barnabas: "We passed a pleasant social day at Colonel Larned's friendly mansion."[35] He responded, "It gives me satisfaction to hear of your employments and amusements. I am glad you have been favored with such agreeable company, as you mention, and should be particularly happy to have been made one of the circle."[36] That was not mere pleasantry, as Barnabas was serious. Mary was maintaining cordial relations with the people who could further Barnabas's career.

Simon Larned was born in 1753, fought in the Revolutionary War, and then settled in Pittsfield in 1784 at the age of thirty-one. He built a house described as "a commodious . . . attractive mansion." He farmed his land and ran a business from his home. Advertisements in the *Pittsfield Sun* newspaper indicate that it was a barter business. Larned traded house ashes and pot ashes for West Indian and European goods, and cotton; he traded wheat for nails.

Larned was civic-minded and served in elected positions, including sheriff; Mary calls him Sheriff. His popularity grew, and in 1806, when the charter was granted for the Berkshire Bank, Larned was named its first president.

It is at this propitious moment that Mary comes to Pittsfield to call and adds, "Mrs. Danforth returned with me to the Sheriff's where we drank tea together."[37]

Larned was anxious to increase his fortune, and so in 1809, with James Colt, Elkanah Watson, and Joshua Danforth, he founded the Pittsfield Wool and Cotton Factory. The fates of the bank and the factory were intertwined because the bank funded the factory.

All the Berkshire Bank directors were local men, but the moving force behind the bank was a Bostonian named Andrew Dexter. The same year the factory opened, there were no fewer than fifty lawsuits filed against Berkshire Bank. All were actions brought by Berkshire County residents attempting to get their money back, but there was no money in the bank. The total deposits in the bank, $80,000, had disappeared. The bank failure wiped away the financial support for the factory, and it failed.

Although Andrew Dexter and the $80,000 disappeared at the same time and were never seen again, the court held the local bank directors—Hurlbut, Colt, Danforth, Larned, and Stockbridge innkeeper Pepoon—responsible. They could not repay the money, and so their property was seized, sold, and paid to the account holders as partial recompense.

The Court sold Larned's property to the Bank of Columbia in 1810, and Pepoon's inn at Stockbridge in 1812 for $12. In 1816 the Bank of Columbia sold Larned's land and mansion to John B. Root and John Hunt (Larned's son-in-law). In 1826, Root and Hunt sold Larned's property to Nathan Willis.

Larned and the other directors were jailed in Lenox. During the whole of his incarceration, Larned retained the position of Pittsfield sheriff. He also retained the respect of people of Pittsfield. Regardless of the court finding, Pittsfield never blamed Larned or the other directors. Pittsfield as a community blamed the Bostonian Andrew Dexter.

When Larned was set free, he rejoined the military as a captain and fought in the War of 1812. With him on the battlefield was his son Charles. Larned died in Pittsfield in 1817 without his land or his "commodious mansion." And yet . . .

Nathan Willis, the new owner, came to Pittsfield in 1814 when he was fifty years old. He owned and operated Nathan Willis & Son, a general store, on Bank Row. In 1823, Charles Larned married Lucy Willis, Nathan's daughter, and in 1849, the couple moved into Larned House and thus restored the "friendly," "attractive," and "commodious mansion" to the family that built it.

Mary did not live to see her friend jailed but she would have understood how, as Larned languished in jail, he retained his position as sheriff. It sounds like a joke. However, the vicissitudes of fate can be mitigated by social position, family connections, and one's social circle. Without those things one can be tossed around brutally. Mary understood; Barnabas would learn.

> *Cousin Isaac Spring left us this morning. We have been much grati-*
> *fied with his visit. He appears to be a worthy man, and possesses*
> *more information than I should, from his limited advantages, imag-*
> *ine. His heart seems deeply impressed with a sense of gratitude to you.*
> *He entreated me to present his respects to you, and his ardent wishes,*
> *that your benevolent exertions for the poor Africans might be suc-*
> *cessful, persuaded of your patriotism, and many excellencies, he hopes*
> *your efforts for the general good will not intermit. Col. Williams, Mr.*
> *A Williams, Mr. Walker, and Mr. Phelps, have all called on me since*
> *I last wrote, and each request respectful salutations to your honor.*[38]

Stockbridge, December 16, 1806: "Yesterday Mama, Sally and your old rib drank tea with Mrs. and Miss Edwards. I have never seen the Squire [Timothy Edwards] more courteous, attentive and agreeable. Polite enquires for you were not omitted. Burr [Vice President of the United States Aaron Burr Jr.] had mentioned in a letter to his sister your calling upon Mr. Dubois.[39]

In September 1807 Mary wrote, "Soon may the pen of another record mine [her death]": how prescient and how sad. Mary died four months later; what remained were a portrait, a memory of a life well spent, and her letters. How might she have recorded what happened next? How might she have mitigated it?

In an age when men's and women's roles were so clear and distinct—when the man was the protector and defender of home and family—ironically, Barnabas was being protected by Mary.

Political Intrigue

> *Barnabas Bidwell's life did not exactly spin out of control when*
> *his wife Mary Gray Bidwell died suddenly in February 1808. But*
> *without knowing it he had suddenly become more vulnerable to the*
> *tides of political fortune.*[40]

He was in Boston when the letter arrived: Mary was sinking. He grabbed a horse and rode. It is 135 miles from Boston to Stockbridge. A horse went along at about six miles an hour. He could whip the animal up to ten miles an hour, but he could not sustain it. However fast Barnabas rode, it was not fast enough. When he arrived at the corner of Pine and Plain, the doors and windows at The Elms stood open. It was February but "the doors stood open in the New England custom of airing out the smell of the cadaver."[41] Or was it honoring the more ancient Indian custom of letting the spirit escape? For the next several days, every eulogy or description of events had Barnabas "bathed in tears."

— ⁓ —

The deaths of three women severed Barnabas's connection to the Sedgwick household and interrupted cordial relations with his political rivals: Pamela Dwight Sedgwick died in September 1807, and Mary Gray Bidwell died on February 1, 1808. "Humbly confiding in the mercy of God, through the atonement of the Savior, with patience and pious resignation for the expected call from the eternal world."[42] Mary's mother and Pamela's Aunt Gray, Sarah Spring Gray, died in October of 1809.

The fine points of the scandal were debated for the next twenty-four years until his death in 1833. Whatever the truth of the matter, whatever the totality of contributing factors, after those deaths, the life of Barnabas Bidwell was changed forever.

Barnabas Bidwell (1761–1833) was the second son of a country preacher. He was smart and articulate, with looks that neither compelled nor repelled. He was educated at Yale, which every eighteenth-century man should have done if only he could, unless he was at Harvard.

His father, the Reverend Adonijah Bidwell, died when Barnabas was twenty-one and still at Yale. His mother, Jemima Devotion Bidwell, died when he was a boy of eight. Barnabas was an orphan and the second son of a Congregational minister in a township without a name. He was a smart man on a campus of smart men. The only thing that distinguished Barnabas was his ambition.

Barnabas graduated from Yale College. He was admitted to the Connecticut bar in 1790. He practiced law briefly, lightly contemplated a

Sarah Spring Gray
COURTESY OF THE BIDWELL HOUSE MUSEUM, MONTEREY, MASSACHUSETTS

career in teaching, and seriously looked around for a mentor. He chose the "Duke of Stockbridge": a sobriquet that correctly identified Judge Theodore Sedgwick as a formidable political power in Berkshire County.

Sedgwick was a staunch Federalist with an impeccable resume. He was a representative to the Continental Congress, and a favorite of George Washington. He served in the Massachusetts State Senate and the US Congress. After he was named Speaker of the US House of Representatives, it was a short step to the US Senate, and President Pro Tem. His last appointment was to the Massachusetts Supreme Judicial Court. One would say Sedgwick had a secure political position if that were not an oxymoron.

Sedgwick ushered Barnabas into his law office, and into Massachusetts politics. Interesting how closely Barnabas's career mirrored Sedgwick's. Barnabas also served in the state house, and the US House of Representatives. He returned to Massachusetts to serve the law, not in

Superior Court but as Attorney General. Perhaps those were the stepping stones for a politically ambitious young man; perhaps Sedgwick advised him. They had in common being self-made men. For a time they also had in common allegiance to the Federalist Party.

Then the plot thickens, though no one (certainly not Barnabas) noticed. Beginning in 1791, Barnabas served as Berkshire County Treasurer.[43] Apparently in the absence of any other willing candidate, he continued to serve as treasurer for almost twenty years. Simultaneously with being treasurer he was a representative in Boston and a member of the US House of Representatives in Washington. He didn't notice the plot thickening; he barely noticed the obligation. He rarely entered the treasurer's offices and used clerks to manage the day-to-day responsibilities. It was such a negligible position in Barnabas's scheme of things, an obligation so lightly regarded. Odd that it would destroy his life.

As a Federalist, Barnabas was ardent, just not constant. It appears that the violence of Shays' Rebellion[44] fought in the Berkshire's backyard bound him to the party. It may be that sincere respect for Thomas Jefferson lured him away or it may be that an ambitious man seized the propitious moment. Whichever it was, overnight, this unknown became a "who's that guy?" by publishing a response to a letter published by Sedgwick.

The back story is this: When Sedgwick decided to retire from Congress, he wrote a letter to the newspapers. It was a sort of summing up, a salute to the accomplishments of his party, the Federalist Party. Bidwell's response was vitriolic. "… a solid majority will eventually oppose and crush them [the Federalists] And blessed be God that day appears to be fast approaching."[45]

Not friendly, but Barnabas was not content to leave it there. He attacked Sedgwick personally as sadly out of touch and absurd. Recall that the man he was attacking was a family member, neighbor, mentor, established politician who gave young Barnabas his start—remember that—because Barnabas did not.

When Aaron Burr and Thomas Jefferson were vying for the office of president of the United States, the decision was in the hands of the Electoral College. When, after the thirty-fifth ballot, Jefferson won, it is alleged that Sedgwick declared, "The gig is up." It is interesting to note that the man who lost the presidency, Aaron Burr, and the man commenting on the loss were both cousins of Mary Gray Bidwell. Sedgwick was right; the loss marked a shift in the balance of power from the Federalists to the Republicans in the country.

Barnabas's political life was greatly enhanced by a timely switch to the Republican Party as well as his personal friendship with Jefferson. A short time after he began serving in Congress, Barnabas became the president's floor manager in the House of Representatives. In 1806, Barnabas Bidwell was one of the most influential political figures in Washington. It was rumored he was being considered for the US Supreme Court to replace his friend Judge Cushman with whom he took tea and supped. He won his second term to Congress and then abruptly took the position as Attorney General in Boston.

It was not a political decision; not the move of an ambitious man. It was the decision of a husband who missed his wife, his hearth and home. In explanation, he said simply that Boston was closer to Stockbridge than Washington.

It was not, however, close enough. When he arrived, in the February frost, the doors and windows stood open and he never saw Mary alive again.

It started immediately in 1808. The Federalists have neither forgiven nor forgotten. They noticed a defalcation in the books of the Treasurer. He was called to explain. The amount missing grew from perhaps $1,000 to $12,000, not in fact but merely in published accounts. The amount was smaller in Republican papers, exponentially larger in Federalist newspapers. New England was still a Federalist stronghold, and in the end Barnabas was indicted. It was 1810, and the Berkshire County Clerk of Courts, Joseph Woodbridge, a Federalist, issued Barnabas's arrest warrant; he had studied law under Judge Sedgwick and married into the family. When the papers were served, it was discovered Barnabas was gone. Gone from his large house on Plain Street, gone from his law office behind, gone from the Attorney General's office in Boston. Barnabas fled to Canada, where he lived out his days. Disbarred, he sat second chair to his son, attorney Marshall Bidwell, and wrote poems to Mary.

They blamed him for that. They said fleeing proved guilt. Those who defended him, however, said it was the wisest course because the

Federalists' political mania, political hunger for control and thirst for retribution, made fair process impossible.

As absolute proof of that, a nephew wrote about the man with the task of arresting Bidwell in a letter introduced with the words: "J. Woodbridge's feelings and conduct toward Uncle Bidwell."[46]

It was Charles Sedgwick, son of the man Bidwell had wronged but also a cousin, who warned him. Woodbridge had been crafty, implying he would send for a warrant when he had one in hand. Luckily Bidwell was in a wagon taking him over the New York state line. Some said the whole affair made Woodbridge unpopular; some said the affair made clear that Bidwell was not a trustworthy or popular man.

No matter what others said about Barnabas Bidwell, before the scandal or after, his Mary said this:

Stockbridge Jan. 13th 1807: Last Friday, my dearest, best friend, I had the unexpected gratification of your affectionate salutation at the commencement of the New Year. Accept in return the warmest gratitude of my heart—a heart truly yours—Yours by every tender and endearing tie! Each returning year has indeed brought me additional cause of tenderness and gratitude—affection for the best of husbands, and gratitude to the Disposer of all events for bestowing such a friend upon a creature so forgetful of His mercies, but who wishes to appreciate as she ought the value of this blessing while it is indulged. Not merely the first, but the labor of my pen on the first day of the year, was devoted to the friend of my heart."[47]

Chapter 6

Women and the Law

A husband is entitled to exercise moderate correction of her [his wife's] behavior. The same as he may do with apprentices and children.[1]

In eighteenth-century New England, there were only two legal positions possible for women—*feme covert* and *feme sole*. Both defined a woman's status in relationship to men. Feme covert, the covered female, referred to a married woman. Feme sole, the woman alone, was an unmarried woman, a widow or spinster or divorcee. There was a third legal delineation, a subset of the other two: deputy husband. If she made legal application, a feme sole or feme covert, could temporarily become a "deputy husband" and exercise the rights usually reserved for men.

Feme Sole

If feme sole, the woman alone, was a spinster, the position could be precarious, even harrowing. If she had no husband to provide a home and sustenance, she was dependent upon some other man—a father, uncle, brother or brother-in-law—for a roof over her head. Since it was assumed that all women wished to be married, the spinster might also be subjected to scorn or pity.

Legally, it seemed better to be a spinster if she could rise above the social stigma. She could hold a job and keep her wages. However, when one looked more closely, a spinster's rights were not actually improved. A single woman of good repute could exercise a "lawful trade or employment" only with the approval of a parent, guardian, and/or town selectman. Other men substituted for a husband in granting rights and permissions.

Only sons inherited, so while there was no legal bar to a spinster owning property there was scant opportunity for her to accumulate any. A widow, however, was in a much different position. Given the right circumstances she could assume some of her husband's rights after his death. Key among those: she could inherit and own his property.

It was said of Madam Williams that she fulfilled best not the role of maiden or wife but the role of widow.

Hannah Dickenson Williams was the third wife of Col. William Williams. Hannah was his wife when he wrote the glowing letter about Pittsfield to her brother Nathaniel.

Hannah Dickenson was born in Deerfield in 1730, the daughter of Samuel and Hannah Field Dickenson. Hannah was a spinster far too long to suit eighteenth-century taste. When they married in 1763, Hannah Dickenson was thirty-three years old and Williams was fifty. It took her some time, but Hannah made a good match.

Williams was born in 1713 and graduated from Harvard in 1729. He joined the military and served until 1748, then resigned and settled in Deerfield as a shopkeeper. In 1752 his aunt, Madam Prudence Stoddard, made his fortune and his future for him. She transferred the proprietorship in Pittsfield to him and with the land and title the responsibility to "bring forth a settlement."[2]

In 1753 he moved to Pittsfield. The French and Indian War loomed, and he again joined the military. He rose to the rank of colonel, and during his life in Berkshire County served as Pittsfield selectman and treasurer, justice of the peace, judge of the Court of Commons Pleas and Probate court judge.

During his more than thirty years as a citizen of Pittsfield, Williams was well liked, well respected, and prosperous. He was described, briefly, as a soldier, a judge, a Tory, and the man who saved the Pittsfield Elm.[3] Williams died in 1785 at the age of seventy-two.

Although Hannah was Williams's third wife, theirs was the longest of his three marriages, lasting twenty-two years. The reason may be that their marriage was childless—both his other wives died in childbirth.

Just six years after Williams's death, on the 1791 tax rolls Hannah was listed as one of the five largest landholders and richest people in Pittsfield.[4] It would be another sixty years before a married woman could legally own and dispose of property separate from her husband's control. Hannah's financial position was possible only because she was a widow.

Major Israel Stoddard, a nephew, described Williams's three marriages this way: "first to Miss Miriam Tyler for her good sense, and got it; second to Miss Sarah Wells for love and beauty, and had it, and third to Aunt Hannah Dickenson and got horribly cheated."

Stoddard did not like Hannah, and probably not many did. A powerful and financially successful woman was an anomaly and not likely to be popular. Still it is not clear in what way Stoddard believed Williams was cheated—in the matter of money or matters of the heart. Williams lived well until he died. Hannah didn't cheat him out of money. Instead she cheated everyone else.

She persuaded Williams to place everything in her name shortly before his death essentially making her a "deputy husband." Therefore, he seemed to die penniless, or specifically to have approximately 175 pounds in his estate. His creditors, holding paper for much larger amounts, were cheated. His children fared no better. His son by his first wife predeceased him. The four children by his second wife were married and settled, which was lucky as there was nothing in the estate for them to inherit. Hannah had it all, and she was not about to share.

The reports about her were not kind and perhaps not true. According to one report, the youngest child, an unmarried daughter, was "turned adrift by William Williams' third wife and joined the Shakers." If all the Williams children were married and settled, how is the story of the suffering of an unmarried daughter true?

Hannah was a spinster long enough to learn the ways of her world, and if she had not persuaded her husband to transfer the property, she may have been at the mercy of a male executor holding her purse strings. Doubtless some were displeased with her business tactics, but she must have garnered the respect of others. She was named executor or administrator of a number of wills—a very unusual position of trust for an eighteenth-century woman.

Two Widows

The man who had given Madam Williams money, power, and control, her husband William Williams, was a probate court judge in 1778. Was he sitting when John Bacon and Edward Higby petitioned for custody of the Deane children?[5] Did the cousin of Ephraim Williams, who grabbed land from the Indians,[6] listen patiently to those who sought to grab land from the Widow Deane? Would he have been sympathetic, granted the petition? On the one hand he was a Tory and anti-Constitutionalist, one of the Connecticut river gods greedy for land. On the other hand he was the husband who had been so liberal with his wife assuring she would be a rich widow. How would he have treated Lavinia? We will never know just because Bacon and Higby applied for guardianship in 1778. The Reverend Allen closed the Berkshire courts from 1775 to 1780. To manage legal matters in county, the process was decentralized. Matters were heard in taverns in the towns and villages. John Fisk, Deacon Bacon, and Edward Higby (yeoman) were heard in the Widow Bingham's tavern by Stockbridge shopkeeper Timothy Edwards.

The Widow Marries

The personality characteristics of a good wife and those of a successful independent woman were perforce very different in eighteenth-century America. The apparently romantic notion of two people becoming one was meant literally in the eighteenth century, obliterating the rights of the woman.

Harmony in the household, not to mention domestic bliss, was achieved when two bodies were joined with but one head. There was need for just one thinker, one decision maker, but four hands. The fruits of the labor of her hands were not her property but his. Neither of those ideals of domestic felicity appealed to Madam Williams, and so there were many to whom Madam Williams did not appeal. On the other hand, she had maneuvered so that henceforth she made all her own decisions and she held onto all the fruits.

For one so adept at widowhood, it is strange that Hannah married again. Her second marriage was to Joseph Shearer, a man twenty-six years her junior. It was possible that both received in the marriage what they bargained for: Joseph needed money and Hannah was charmed by his courting. It is said he told her that he "worshiped the ground she walked on" and since she owned more property than almost anyone else in Pittsfield, he was probably speaking the absolute and unvarnished truth.

Once the bargain was struck, however, no one in Pittsfield confused theirs with a happy marriage. Hannah brought charges against Shearer for plotting her murder. She charged he attempted to kill her by seating her on an unbroken horse, by leaving the cover off a well in hopes she would step into it, and by poisoning her food. The evidence, however, failed to sustain the charge, and Joseph left the court a free man. For any who doubted his innocence, history redeemed him. Or perhaps Hannah bringing charges subdued him, restrained any further efforts. In either case, Joseph did not bury his wife until she was ninety-one.

Her tombstone bore witness to the fact that wife was not the best role for Hannah. The tombstone of Williams's second wife reads: "Here is interred ye agreeable and generous Mrs. Sarah Williams consort of Colonel William Williams who died February 24, 1764, with her infant babe." Hannah's tombstone reads: "To the memory of Madam Hannah Williams consort of the Honorable William Williams and last wife of Joseph Shearer Esq. Born September 20, 1730 and died May 21, 1821."

Joseph lived quite comfortably on Hannah's money for another seventeen years. Reputedly, he was generous to friends, family, and the town of Pittsfield, but Joseph Shearer wasted not one word of affection on his wife's tombstone.

Feme Covert

In 1762 a maiden pondered, "I often run over in my mind the many disadvantages that accrue to our sex from an alliance with the other [a man] but the thought of being doomed to live alone I can't yet reconcile."[7]

It is true that most if not all eighteenth-century women wanted to be married. The question is why?

In the eighteenth century, feme covert meant covered by her husband. Unfortunately there is an element of smothered and disappeared from view about it. It was a law intended for the protection of married women. Mostly it protected a wife from not having any rights at all.

"The legal being and existence of a wife is incorporated into that of her husband under whose protection and cover" she was supposed to live. For his benefit and only with his "allowance and approbation" could a wife do anything.

Marriage was a risky proposition; the couple's future health and welfare, not to mention their social position, depended upon a good choice. The consequences of a bad choice were well known. A poor decision could leave a woman lonely, her children cold and hungry. If her husband were shiftless, profligate, intemperate, or disloyal, there was little she could do even to keep body and soul together.

A goodwife in Vermont sought ownership of the cow. She meant to keep the products of the beast and therefore the profits away from a drunken husband. There was no legal purchase, no avenue, under feme covert for her to claim ownership.

If a man chose unwisely, if his wife were not steady, thrifty, virtuous, and able, his household could fall apart and his children suffer.

Sadly if she married an abuser, a vulgarian, drunkard, slangwhanger (an officious, noisy, demagogue), slugabed (idler), or bindlestiff (wanderer, hobo), she had legal recourse to law but would not find a sympathetic ear or even a sensible solution.

Eighteenth-century women were instructed in church, and in court, if they got that far, that the solution to any marital problem was self-control and personal improvement. Precisely how a woman's reformation corrected incest, adultery, or desertion is not detailed.

The limited grounds upon which a divorce could be granted were bigamy, consanguinity (incest), impotence, and adultery. These grounds were common throughout New England. Some states included desertion but others did not.

The position of a deserted wife in or out of court was intolerable. If she lived in a state that allowed divorce on grounds of desertion, she had to be able to find the man to pursue her rights. If she lived in a state that did not, she was left without means of support or the means to correct the situation. She had neither the personal right to work nor the legal right to divorce.

Divorce *a mensa et thoro* was another legal conclusion that was merely hobbling. It was a legal separation wherein the husband was required to continue to support the wife financially but neither was allowed to remarry.

The upper-class wife, the madam, may be better fed and better dressed than her lower-class counterpart, the goody, but was not necessarily better off. For either woman divorce was almost impossible because both were divorced from justice.

A wife could not run for elected office. A widow or spinster could but she couldn't get elected. She could not vote or hold a job outside the home. If a wife did hold a job, she was not entitled to her wages; they were her husband's just as the fruits of her labors at home were his. She could not serve on a jury, in the military, or in the clergy. She could not have a will (until 1809 in Connecticut and later in other states). She had little need for a will as by law she owned nothing: not property inherited, nor income earned, nor property owned prior to the marriage. All property, real and personal, was owned in common with her husband over which he had sole discretion. Her marriage contract was the last contract she could or would ever sign.

Far from illegal, physical discipline in the home was a responsibility of husbands and fathers. Responsible for a wife's debts and misbehavior, a husband was entitled to exercise "moderate correction of her behavior. The same as he may do with apprentices and children."

Somehow, the subject of murder seems to follow logically. The consequence for the murder of a wife by a husband was identical to the consequence if he had killed a stranger. If a wife killed a husband, however, it was considered treason. The consequence was death by being "drawn and burned alive." It was very far-sighted of the male lawmakers to make the punishment so severe, because the most favorable legal status for an eighteenth-century woman was widow.

She had "dower rights" and must inherit at least a third of the husband's estate. As early as 1633, a widow could administer the husband's estate. If her husband died bankrupt, "the comfort of the widow and children must be considered before the creditors."

Have you ever wondered why early American history more often recounts the stories of men? There are so many primary source materials aside from letters, journals, and diaries. There are church records, town records, the census from 1790 on, Massachusetts tax valuation of 1771, deeds, probate, civil, and criminal court records. All of these sources require one thing: a name. Concomitant with legal anonymity and absence from any role outside the home, married women were nameless. Along with their legal rights, married women in the eighteenth century lost their first and maiden names; they were referred to by their husband's name—Mrs. John Smith.

Until the nineteenth century, these were the laws. It was not until the mid-nineteenth century in New York State that women could "hold property to her separate use." Other states followed. It was late in the twentieth century before there was any legal concept of rape or physical abuse of a wife by a husband. On the other hand, from the earliest days in the colonies, it was illegal to "draw away the affection of any maid with the pretense of marriage before he hath obtained liberty and allowance of the parents."[8] Furthermore "an assault upon any maid in the fields, streets, or lanes or despoiling her or defacing her garments or ornaments"[9] was punished with ten lashes and thirty days in jail. Interesting that assaulting or despoiling in the home was not mentioned.

Deputy Husband

Regardless of the sorrow of a widow or the vulnerability of a divorcee, she gained this: She could keep her own wages, profits, and produce; she could buy, own, sell, will, and inherit property. She could conduct business if anyone would conduct it with her; she could borrow if anyone would lend and lend if anyone would borrow from a woman. Widowed or divorced she had no choice but to try. However, there were other conditions under which a wife would seek the rights of a husband.

If she were the wife of a fisherman or whaler gone to sea for months at a time even though a covered woman she must ask for the rights of her husband in order to survive while he was away. Similarly if a wife were separated or deserted she must appeal for those rights to survive as Fanny Baker did:

> *This is to certify that I Fanny Baker now living in Vergennes have, for two years past, without the help of my husband, Josiah Baker, received my sustenance and support through my own means and having it in my power to continue providing for myself, I take this opportunity through the medium of the public newspaper, of making known my determination of doing as well as I can.*[10]

The rights of a deputy husband were generally granted not because there was a taste for equity, not because the condition was otherwise intolerable, but because these were practical people. If the rights were not granted, the woman could, probably would, become a financial burden on the village. Besides, it was assumed that these rights were granted temporarily and that a good wife would (and would want to) revert to her proper role as soon as practicable.

Divorce

A disobedient clamorous wife . . .[11]

Although a married woman was without property or the legal right to own property, there was an avenue into civil court for her, and that was a petition for divorce. If a woman filled the petition for divorce, the acceptable grounds—consanguinity, bigamy, and sexual incapacity—were those that annulled marriage. "True divorce (*divortium a vinculo matrimonii*) was never granted unless a marriage was judged null to begin with."[12]

Strictly speaking, for a woman, there was no such thing as divorce. On the other hand, Amos Bliss filed for divorce on the grounds that his wife Phoebe "behaved herself unfriendly . . . and [was] wasteful and careless of his provisions and goods."[13]

A man could request an end to the marriage based on his personal dissatisfaction. That was fair grounds because the contract was based upon the wife being subservient, working continually for the husband's benefit and of course, being friendly. In his filing, Amos did mention that he was perfectly willing to drop the whole proceedings and have Phoebe back if "she would be in subjection to me."

Abigail Bailey was married to a man who had "committed incest on the body of his daughter."[14] Still she was in anguish.

> *I persuaded myself that if he would do what was right relative to our property, and would go to some distant place, where we should be afflicted with him no more, it would be sufficient and I should be spared the dreadful scene of prosecuting my husband.*[15]

There was potential anguish but the larger point was that Mrs. Bailey may have attempted and failed to get the divorce.

In her research of the Massachusetts divorce records for the period of 1692 to 1786, Nancy Cott found substantially more than half were applied for in the last twenty years. That is, there were 229 applications filed in the entire period, and 159 applications in the years 1764–1786. The total number of applications was almost 50/50—128 women applied and 101 men. Cott concludes that throughout the eighteenth century, there was a dramatic increase in the desire for dissolution of marriage. "Most likely," Cott writes, "divorce petitions increased not because spouses more often had legitimate grievances but because they were more often motivated to respond to marital wrongs by seeking divorce."

There is, however, more to the story. There were rents in the fabric, a change in the overarching conditions. The hierarchy was breaking down. The likelihood of being granted the divorce for which a man or wife petitioned increased. More petitions filed by women were being granted. As both men and women observed that there was an increasing chance of success, more were motivated to try. In 1792 Mrs. Bailey was granted a divorce on the grounds of consanguinity.

Crimes

> *Be it enacted . . . that if any man shall forcibly and without consent ravish any maid or woman by committing carnal copulation with*

*her against her consent, he shall be put to death. Provided complaint
and prosecution be made forthwith upon the rape.*[16]

Criminal conduct is divided between crimes against property and crimes
against persons. The legal standing of a woman, feme sole or feme covert,
was considered so negligible that "The Acts and Laws of His Majesty's
Colony of Connecticut in New England in America 1750—1771" only
considered it possible to commit a crime against a woman's body.

Fornication

*Court of General Sessions: "Berkshire Anno Reggie Regis George
Tetra Dei Gratis Magne Britannica" (In this year of the most regal
King George the 4h God grace/bless Great Britain.)*

In 1761 Berkshire was considered sufficiently settled and civilized to
become a county, and to have a criminal court. It was called the Court of
General Sessions.

The first case heard in the Court of General Sessions on September
1, 1761, was that of "Susannah York of Sheffield who confesses herself
guilty of the crime of fornication on the ninth day of April Anno Domini
1760 and the court having considered of her offense ordered that she pay
as a fine to the King the sum of 13/4 and she paid the costs accordingly."

The justices sitting that day were Joseph Dwight, William Williams, John Ashley, and Timothy Woodbridge. They fined York because
her crime was "against the peace, authority, and dignity of the commonwealth." The value of the fine exacted, 13 shillings 4 pence, was equal to
the value of two deer skins—not an insignificant sum. Yet it was seemingly the least of the penalties available.

According to the colonial laws of Massachusetts, "the court had the
authority and could order therefore that if any man commit fornication
with any single woman they [both of them] shall be punished either by
enjoining marriage or fine or corporal punishment or all or any of these
as the judges of the court that hath cognizance of the cause shall appoint."
A later amendment added disenfranchisement as a punishment "for this
shameful and vicious crime."[17]

In every court session from 1761 to 1795 there was at least one for-nication case. Interestingly, only women came forward and admitted to the act—no men. If accused, far fewer men than women were convicted. One can imagine all sorts of reasons for the uneven application of justice, but the truth is that a woman was convicted when she was unmarried and pregnant or "a single woman who was begotten of a Bastard Child born of her body." The pregnancy and child were proofs positive of the act. In the eighteenth century there were few ways to prove paternity. Still, one wonders, did anyone think these women committed this particular crime alone?

Men were presented before the court and admitted to other moral infractions. In 1760 and 1761 Samuel Lee "did keep an inn and house of entertainment in his dwelling contrary to the law of this province." Mr. Root, a tavern keeper, "suffered dancing in his tavern." One man "labored and did his ordinary calling [on Sunday] therefore profaned the Lord's Day." Unlike women, men if accused of fornication could simply deny it.

For example, Thankful Purcey appeared and "confessed to have been guilty of the crime of fornication within the body of the county on or about the latter end of the month of July or the beginning of the month of August A.D. 1760." Unlike other women, Purcey returned to court to name her partner and bring suit against him in the amount of 10 pounds—a prodigious sum.

Nathaniel Reynolds and Ezra Hiccock stood surety (put up the 10 pounds) for Charles Miller, the man named. If Miller should lose the case to Purcey, "then the aforesaid Nathaniel and Ezra shall pay the cost that has or may arise from said complaint."

For the balance of the year and the year following, the matter did not come before the court. Apparently Miller denied the complaint, and the case fell apart. Was there no way to prove the man's complicity in a world before DNA tests?

Actually the eighteenth-century world had a plan. On January 28, 1762, Amy Coleman of Pittsfield brought a complaint against David Roberts of Pittsfield and won. "The spinster preformed prerequisites of the law to entitle her to support for the child—3 shillings per week paid quarterly." The prerequisites of law that Coleman performed were to name the father in the hearing of the midwife during labor. During labor, the midwife repeatedly asked any unmarried mother to identify the father. It was believed that any answer given during "her travail" was the truth because during labor, she was facing death, and therefore would not dare lie. Even if the man denied the charge, when the woman repeatedly gave the same name during labor, and the midwife testified in court to what she heard, the man was convicted.

Miller probably succeeded with a simple denial because Purcey either did not become pregnant or did not come to term and deliver a child thus eliminating the only paternity test accepted in the eighteenth century. Furthermore, if Purcey did not give birth, the court was disinclined to pursue the case.

The reason is apparent in the second part of the ruling in the case of Coleman. In addition to money paid to support mother and child, the father was ordered to "pay to Pittsfield the sum of 200 pounds in lawful money to save and spare the town of Pittsfield from any charge that might hereafter arise by reason of said child being born." Prosecution of fornication cases had as much to do with money as morality.

Eighteenth-century Berkshire was a series of small communities: knots of as few as 138 families, or fewer, living in wide clearings in the woods connected by narrow dirt roads. They were vulnerable. Fatherless children were a potential financial burden on the community. The court was making sure that the responsible party paid thus "easing of the towns where bastards are born [the cost] of the child and the education thereof."

It was not only fatherless children that the community feared were a threat to their financial well-being. They also feared strangers—any who "have lately come here to reside and not been duly admitted." If these newcomers could not demonstrate familial connections with settled members of the community, or if their economic circumstances could not be determined to be sound, they were warned out. That is, the court was empowered to find them and give them formal notice of a date by which they had to leave.

There was one last financial interest in the fornication trials. In 1762, Sarah Joyner of Egremont "was brought to answer" a charge of fornication made by members of the community. Since she did not come forward of her own accord, when she was found guilty, her fine was larger: 20 shillings 4 pence.

Joyner could not pay the fine and therefore was to "stand committed till that sentence be performed." In such a case, anyone could come forward and pay the fine. By virtue of payment, Sarah was bonded to that person until she repaid the debt. So the fines were only seemingly the least of the punishments. If they went unpaid, in the eighteenth century, premarital sex was a possible road to slavery.

Sarah returned to the court in an effort to name the father and force him to pay the fine. In *Joyner v. Joseph Taylor* heard by John Apley, Esq., Justice of the Peace, Taylor was ordered "to make his personal appearance here at this time to answer to a complaint of said Sarah against him that said Joseph wherein she charges him of having carnal knowledge of her said Sarah and begating a bastard child on her body."

James Smith and Abraham Root stood surety, and "now recognized anew in the sum of 50 pounds" and swore they too would appear personally at the next court of General Sessions."

The next time the court conveyed "at Pittsfield for and within our county of Berkshire on the first Tuesday next" Taylor was to be "present to answer to said complaint and to perform the judgment of said court thereon and not depart without license [permission of the court]."

Without explanation, Joseph Taylor of Sheffield, at the aforementioned court session, "is now discharged from his said recognizance in due form of law."

Statutory Rape

Be no flatterer; neither play with any that delights not to be played with.[18]

The consequences of what we would call statutory rape, and other unregulated sexual behavior, were far reaching. An act that took place in 1761 was still affecting a family one hundred years later.[19]

In 1861, a man sat down to write a letter to his daughter. She was the last remaining member of his immediate family. His wife Eliza Lamson

Campbell died five months earlier, and his four sons and one other daughter were "lying by the side of their mother in the burying grounds."

"Feeling my infirmities and that I might soon be taken away," Stanton Archibald Campbell wrote his one remaining child, Truth Alice Campbell: "to leave for her benefit a brief record or history of her family and relations." Campbell was forty-four years old; his daughter was nine.

It was a loving sentiment and useful letter. It told a daughter about to be left alone in the world who and where her relations were; who among them might be enjoyed and trusted; whom it might be better to avoid. It was also a truthful letter. Perhaps inspired by his daughter's name, it told her both the rough and the smooth about her family members. For example, one Lamson aunt "married a man although she had one child before she was married. He of course is a low ignorant man or he would not have married her."

Now here was sauce for the historian: a letter written by a man about his own family. It would be rich in information with no unanswered questions, no necessity for hours of research. Sadly that is never the case. Human memory is imperfect, human knowledge incomplete. Gaps must be filled—facts checked.

For example, Campbell wrote that his Uncle Archibald "was called out as a soldier I think in the War of 1812. Upon reflection I think it was the Revolutionary War." Uncle Archibald was born in Mt. Washington in 1766. That meant he was nine years old at the onset of the Revolutionary War and forty-six years old in 1812. At either age, it was strange if he were "called out as a soldier," and what exactly did "called out" mean when there was no draft?

The Revolutionary War did not end until 1783, and during that war, it was common parlance to be "called out" by the militia. A search of Revolutionary War records discovered Uncle Archibald. Archibald Campbell was sworn in at Sheffield October 14, 1781, at the age of fifteen. He served in the militia of Colonel Ashley, Mum Bett's owner, as a fifer for ten days during which time he marched to Saratoga.

Other references to Uncle Archibald were more tantalizing to contemplate and more difficult to research. Uncle Archibald "had one child by a girl by the name of Kline who afterward married a man named John

Jones . . . the child was called after his father and he always called my father 'Uncle' but his father never owned him."

Uncle Archibald, father of an illegitimate child, was of Scotch descent, had red hair, and a red-hot temper. He could be cruel to animals, frightened children, and was often morose. Late in life, this singular fellow married a good-natured widow "with whom he lived very happily having his own way in everything. He died in his eighties."

Campbell also wrote details about Uncle Archibald's illegitimate child. Archibald Jr., born in Mt. Washington in 1802, "resembled [his father] physically and in disposition. Cousin Archibald accumulated considerable property and moved with his family from Mt. Washington to New York." How did he accumulate property? If Uncle Archibald would not acknowledge his son, he would support him.

As a young man, Archibald Jr. married into the wealthy and prominent family of Miles Curtis—not once but twice. He married Luana Curtis and when she died, Archibald Jr. married her sister Fanny. With the Curtis sisters, Archibald Jr. had four children—Fanny, Harry, Polly, and Curtis. Probate court records show that in 1826 Miles Curtis left his considerable estate to his son Willis and son-in-law Archibald Jr. as guardian of his four grandchildren.

Campbell wrote his daughter almost nothing about the mother of Archibald Jr.—"a girl by the name of Kline." Why was she dismissed? What was her full name? Why did he call her a girl and not a woman; how old was she when the illegitimate child was born? Was there a fornication trial, and if not, why not?

In 1774 there were only twenty-three families who petitioned for proprietorship of the proposed new town of Mt. Washington. In 1802 when Archibald Jr. was born, Mt. Washington had a population of barely 400. According to General Court records, the Klines, the Campbells, the Curtises, and the Joneses were near neighbors. It was a small population removed by several miles from any larger town with four families clustered together. There was a rich mix for intrigue. In the same General Court records, however, there was no fornication trial involving Uncle Archibald or a girl named Kline. Who was she?

Was there a Kline girl born in a year that made her old enough to mother a child in 1802 and who also married one John Jones? John and

Deidamia Kline married in 1782. They had six children: three boys and three girls. Two of the daughters were too young to be a mother in 1802: Betsy, born in 1800, was two, and Deidamia, born in 1809, was seven. Neither married a man named Jones: Betsy married Willis Curtis; Deidamia married Cyrus Lamson. The third Kline girl was born in 1786 and is listed only as an unnamed female child. She would have been sixteen in 1802, but did she marry a Jones?

In the Mt. Washington Center Cemetery, one inscription reads: "John Jones died 1846; his wife Elizabeth Kline Jones died 1843, and this stone set by their youngest son B. A. Jones."

The mother of Archibald Campbell Jr. was Elizabeth Kline Jones, born 1786, the daughter of John and Deidamia Kline, and the sister-in-law of Willis Curtis and Cyrus Lamson, which made her both a sister-in-law and an aunt to her own son. When Archibald Jr. was conceived, Elizabeth was sixteen years old; Uncle Archibald was thirty-four.

Elizabeth was certainly at a disadvantage, being pursued by a thirty-four-year-old man. The question is: Was Elizabeth a minor or had she reached the age of consent? Sadly, according to the law, any girl over the age of ten was deemed capable of sexual consent.[20]

Elizabeth married John Jones in 1802, the year Archibald Jr. was born. The marriage in the same year as the illegitimate birth explained why there was no fornication trial. The marriage regularized the birth.

What of Elizabeth and John Jones's lives? John purchased his first piece of land in Mt. Washington in 1800 when he was just nineteen. He married Elizabeth when she was sixteen and he was twenty-one. After the birth of Archibald Jr., with John, Elizabeth had seven more children. John purchased additional land in 1803 and 1813. Together John and Elizabeth prospered. All seven children are named in John's will filed in 1846. Elizabeth and John were rich in children who lived to adulthood, and an estate that mentioned, among other treasures, "a mansion house in Mt. Washington."

Research into public records told us much about a sentence fragment in an old letter: "a girl by the name of Kline." Yet there is much we will never know: the circumstances surrounding carnal knowledge of a sixteen-year-old girl by a thirty-four year-old man; the reason John Jones married Elizabeth; why, when by that marriage the birth was regularized, they named the child Archibald Campbell Jr.; why the Campbell family acknowledged the child; why the father did not; and why Stanton Campbell called one man a "low ignorant man" for marrying a woman who had previously borne a child but wrote not one word of criticism about John Jones. We can only guess, and guessing is a disservice to the heroes and villains of the piece.

Prostitution

A majority of the employed women, therefore worked at jobs that were an extension of the feminine sphere.[21]

These jobs in the feminine sphere seemed to be sewing, cooking, housekeeping, nursing, teaching children, and copulating. There was little if any prostitution in the rural areas. There is ample evidence that there were ladies of the night in cities. The countryside was not necessarily more chaste or Arcadian. There was simply less ready cash, almost no discretionary income.

Probably it was for the best. Only 6 percent of the population was in cities, so fewer were exposed to the punishment for prostitution. The Court of General Sessions in Boston issued an order for corporal punishment for a madame. Corporal punishment was no joke. The woman who ran a bawdy house in Boston was administered thirty lashes and then tied to the back of a hand cart and dragged through the town to the sea and then the gallows.

Rape

The caveat was that the maid or woman reports this crime immediately. The other problem was that she was not always believed. It was not so much the men—the judge and jury—who remained unconvinced. It was other women. Elizabeth Goodall was raped by John Smith. She intended to report the crime, but advised by some not to, "she did forebear."[22]

Well, she had discussed to the point of exhaustion and so to put it mildly word got out. The magistrate called her to appear, perhaps suspecting fornication. She told her story and apologized for speaking freely but thought the womenfolk would have held their tongues. She then placed all power to determine truth and punishment squarely in the hands of the magistrate, saying she hoped the man would suffer no more than he deserved. She was believed, and Smith was whipped.

On the other hand, Mary Jenkins claimed she was "forced by John White" and was not believed.

"Were you sensible when the tinker was in the very act?"

"No," Mary said. However, she knew by what he said and circumstances after that she had been raped.

"Did he lie with you after you came out of your fit?"

"No," Mary said.

"For you said he did not lie with you before your fit nor after your fit and in your fit you were not sensible he lay with you."[23]

The court concluded that he never lay with her at all.

The demand that a woman be utterly unconscious during a rape in order to prove noncompliance remained an obstacle to convicting a rapist into the twentieth century.

Criminal Conversation

Criminal conversation was the eighteenth-century term for adultery. In marriage, sexual intercourse was called intimate conversation; outside of an extant marriage it was criminal conversation; and before marriage any and all conversation was denied.

In strict adherence to law, the punishment for a woman convicted of adultery was death. It was so severe that as a practical matter, the charge was rarely if ever brought to criminal court. As a practical matter, just as in the case of *Dexter v. Stoddard*,[24] the matter was brought first to the church and then perhaps to civil court. As with the Widow Deane case, the behavior of the woman was of no particular interest. It could of course be grounds for divorce but that was a different legal proceeding. In Civil Court it was a matter between men: the husband sued the lover for damages. The lover had despoiled his wife and thereby damaged his property.

At times the proof that his mate had "unwifed" him was merely his suspicion based upon an alteration in the way she treated him. Alternately proof may be the hard fact of "French pox" (venereal disease). Then the husband made two claims: she had transmitted it to him; she could only do so if another man had given it to her, and he could not have been the carrier because he had never transgressed.

There was a role for a woman's social circle in these cases. Older women in the community were important actors in stories of criminal conversation. "The mothers" might act as guardians of village morality and report a younger woman's behavior to authorities. Equally, however, they could act as guardian of the younger woman. An older woman, in good standing, was a powerful witness. Her testimony was generally believed just as a midwife was believed in a fornication trial.

In one case a man of high repute accosted a young wife when her husband was away. When she went to an official and reported his "lewd behavior," the official refused to act against a "gentleman." The young wife went to the older women for advice. They believed that she had been prevailed upon and that the gentleman's behavior had been improper. When two older women went together to the official and a case before him, an action in law was forced. The man was punished.

The severe penalties required that the strategies for countering any accusation were swift and clever. In one case, the husband accused the wife of adultery based upon the proof of venereal disease. He complained to his minister and to her father. To the father he refused to ever live with her again. The father acted quickly. Using the letter as proof of desertion, he filed for divorce on this daughter's behalf. It was granted thus minimizing the possibility for a case of criminal conversation. The church simultaneously excommunicated her for lewd behavior and unclean acts: sad surely but a far cry from hanging.

Perhaps the cleverest were those women who used feme covert as their defense. When accused of adultery they did not demur. They admitted the act and placed the blame on their husbands. He was responsible for regulation of the household and the activities within it. She owed him service, but he owed her protection. If he could not satisfy her for any of a variety of reasons, sexual behavior was not regulated within the marriage. He had not protected her, the weaker one, from her passions; in short, he was not a man. He had not fulfilled his part of the bargain; therefore, vulnerable because of her innate weakness, she was forced by his incompetence to break her part. As one-sided as the laws were, as unequal the relationships, ultimately responsibility was deemed commensurate with authority; the supremacy of the male made him the responsible party, and this argument generally succeeded.

Contraception

Contraception was against the law. Fertility and femininity were inexorably linked. The need for children to populate an empty land and work the vast fields was too great to entertain the notion of selective procreation. The death rate among women associated with the birth rate might have generated—at least—discussion, but the belief was strong that such matters were in the hands of God.

The women shared secrets and old wives' tales. For example, it was believed that for the time a woman was nursing she was infertile. The only way that would have been true was if while nursing she said to her husband, "Will you please go away now."

One hundred and fifty years later, in 1912, contraception was still against the law. Margaret Sanger was jailed periodically for her view that a woman had the right to choose and should have a child only when it was the product of a loving relationship, when she consciously desired a child, and when the child could be brought into a situation that assured its health. Contraception was made legal in 1965.

There Is a Tide

It was 1975 before it was considered a crime for a husband to beat his wife. It was two decades into the twentieth century before women were given the right to vote. It was the late nineteenth century before rape was considered a crime. Even then, in 1898, there was a caveat. The woman had to prove she was raped while also swearing that she was unconscious during the act. Objecting, saying no, or even fighting back was not sufficient to establish a crime.

It was the end of the nineteenth century before the age of consent was raised, and it was no longer considered legal, or even possible, for a girl of ten years old to grant permission to an adult male to have sexual intercourse. It was the mid-nineteenth century before married women could hold property individually and separately from their husbands. Even when it was acknowledged that the property belonged to the wife individually, the husband had the right to manage it.

These laws, or the absence of law, were based upon English common law developed in the twelfth century. In turn English common law was built on the belief that a patriarchal society was the natural order of things. Both equality of the sexes and female supremacy were unnatural, against the word of God and the laws of man.

To prevent imposition on the masses by a religious group, a military organization, a king, or a dictator, the Constitution of the United States was written and defended on the battlefield. Men fought to be free of oppression and women seemed to stir. They asked, perhaps tentatively, if they too might free themselves from the imposition of men, from domestic oppression.

Abigail Adams told her husband that "all men would be tyrants if they could." The paragraph in its entirety is slightly less passive and polite than "remember the ladies" appears. It is worth remembering more than the first three words:

> *March 31, 1776, Abigail Adams to John Adams: Remember the ladies, and be more generous and favorable to them than your ancestors. Do not put such unlimited power into the hands of the husbands. Remember all men would be tyrants if they could. If particular care and attention is not paid to the ladies we are determined to foment a Rebellion, and will not hold ourselves bound by any Laws in which we have no voice, or representation.*

In the midst of the American Revolution, the revolution in women's lives was about issues as intimate as a kiss goodnight. It took place at the hearthside, quiet as the hissing flames, delicate as tea cups, well mannered as Abigail Adams's letters, but persistent.

Chapter 7

Women and War

Whatever else is said about eighteenth-century America, this should be remembered: Everything happening in the street, the church, or at home was happening in the context of war. From the French and Indian War to Shays' Rebellion there was war for half a century. These were not foreign wars. The colonists were not reading about them at the tavern, shaking their heads, and ordering another round. These wars were fought outside their door.

On April 4, 1776, Asa Bement bore witness to events. "On Timothy Edwards' return [to Stockbridge from Lansborough], at about 4 o'clock p.m., five men attempted to stop him by violence—one laying ahold of his coat, another [grabbed] his horse's bridle. He disengaged himself by striking a blow with his whip and by the speed of his horse." As he sped away, the men armed with clubs and hoes struck at him "hitting his horse's withers and shouting Tory. Of enormities of this kind, we feel it our duty to give you the earliest notice."[1]

You can almost hear the outrage in Bement's voice but also the trepidation. Violence was on the road you took to market; cannon fire was within earshot; and the enemy was the red-coated soldier but also the Tory next door.

From King Philip's War in the seventeenth century to the War of 1812 in the nineteenth, America was a battle ground. The eighteenth-century wars in order of occurrence were: the French and Indian, 1754–1763; Revolutionary, 1775–1783; and Shays' Rebellion, 1786–1787. Women had a role in each.

The Archetype

The roles of women were various and surprising. Dressed up as men or just hitching up their skirts, women fought. They were also spies, dispatchers, mistresses, camp followers, and wives defending their homes. Sarah Deming was such a wife in Pittsfield before and during the French and Indian War. When her husband left her alone, she defended herself and her home against marauding Indians. The tribesmen intended to take women and children captive to replace those tribe members killed by the settlers but also to scare the settlers off the land. Yet the story of women as warriors does not start with Deming or with the French and Indian War. It starts almost half a century earlier, with Hannah Dustin.[2]

When his farm was attacked, Thomas Dustin, Hannah's husband, ran for his barn. He mounted his horse, and keeping his horse between the Indians and his wife and children, he yelled "Run! Run for the garrison."

He fired and shielded their retreat and yelled, "Run!"

It was 1697, the 15th day of March [at seven a.m.] that the town of Haverhill in Massachusetts was attacked by Indians and some prisoners were there taken . . . among them the intrepid Hannah Dustin.[3]

In the dark of night, when the Indians stopped to rest, Hannah enlisted the help of Mary Neff and a boy named Samuel Lennardson. Hannah took up a tomahawk as did the other two and while the Indians slept, two women and a boy killed their captors.

Mary and the boy wanted to be away, but Hannah refused to leave without their scalps. It was neither anger nor retribution; it was proof of her action. For the practical New England woman, the scalps were a prize she could and did exchange for a cash reward. The General Court in Boston gave a bounty for Indian kills, and a woman would require proof to collect. Legend has it that she patiently cut and carried away twelve Indian scalps.

A few days later her husband traveled to the General Court in Boston on Hannah's behalf:

Haverhill JOHN WARNER BARBER, *HISTORICAL COLLECTIONS*, 1841, P. 183

*To the Right Honorable the Lieut Governor & the Great & General
assembly of the Province of Massachusetts Bay now convened in Boston.*

*The humble petition of Thomas Durstan of Haverhill showeth that
the wife of ye petitioner (with one Mary Neff) hath in her late
captivity among the barbarous Indians, been disposed & assisted
by heaven to do an extraordinary action, in the just slaughter of so
many of the barbarians, as would by the law of the Province which
a few months ago, have entitled the actors unto considerable recom-
pense from the Public.[4]*

Thomas goes on to explain that he lost his "estate in the calamity
wherein his wife was carried into her captivity." He contends that this loss
makes him "more fit to receive what bounty the court deems proper." He
received 25 pounds.

Why start in the seventeenth century? Because Hannah was the
archetype. Feted and sermonized by the Reverend Cotton Mather,[5] her
name was celebrated and so were her twin characteristics. The Church
sanctioned and sang the praises of one who received payment for a righteous deed even when that deed was violent and even when the violent
deed was done by a woman. It was license for the women who came after
Hannah to act as men did in extremis.

Women in the French and Indian War[6]

During the French and Indian War, women coped and survived in a variety of ways. When women feared they might be attacked by Indians while in the barnyard milking, they pushed their hair into men's caps, donned trousers, and leaned muskets beside their pails and stools. When Indians did approach, they fired repeatedly until the Indians retreated into the woods.[7] Similarly when a woman was left alone at night with a baby, she too hefted a gun and fired at advancing Indians.

There is more than one version of the following story. In this telling there was a brutal attack in Stockbridge at a house on the hill. It was the summer of 1755 and the Indians attacked "on Sabbath noon while many of the inhabitants were still at church."[8] Inside the house, while Mrs. John Chamberlain tried to shield her infant, "the father in his fright jumped out of the window and fled."[9] The infant and a three-year-old were bludgeoned to death. Two older boys hid under the bed and between the straw and the feathers on top of the bed and survived the attack.

Owen, a hired servant, was more faithful than the husband and father. He stayed and tried to defend Mrs. Chamberlain. He fought and fell. He was discovered on the floor wounded. They carried him to a neighboring house where he was treated. Mrs. Chamberlain survived; Owen did not.

In 1764, nine years after the event, John Chamberlain sold the sixteen acres with a dwelling house and a blacksmith shop to Asa Bement. It was far enough out of town so that it was evidently a vulnerable location. Bement also saw violence done outside his door, but he was witness, not victim, and survived unscathed.

There were the women with muskets and milking pails and there was Mrs. Chamberlain. On the other hand, when Mary Storer was taken captive and marched by Indians to a French fort near Montreal, she was not displeased with her surroundings. They compared favorably with "the privations of dreary New England."[10] She married a French officer named Jean St. Germaine. In an effort to win his daughter back, her father left 50 pounds[11] in his will to be given to her only if she returned to New England. She did not. Madame St. Germaine lived out her days happily in New France.

The Revolutionary War

The common pests of society and incurable enemies of their country
—J. A. E. SMITH

The Revolutionary War lasted for eight years—eight long years of fighting. You can praise the principles "worth fighting for" that led to the Revolutionary War and you can idealize the resulting changes; you can honor the country that emerged, but still the people had to endure and survive the dangers and upheaval of war.

Between 7 and 10 p.m. on December 16, 1773, patriots poured tea into the harbor at Boston. The notion that the country and all its citizens acted as one, acted enthusiastically, or acted at all is myth. In January 1774, Pittsfield responded:

> *A meeting of the said town may be called to consider the management*
> *and behavior of a number of disguised persons who entered onboard*
> *the vessels in which tea belonging to the honorable East India Com-*
> *pany was shipped lying in the harbor of Boston; then and there hoist-*
> *ing up the chests in which it was contained and shoving the chests*
> *and emptying the tea into the sea; all of which conduct is by these*
> *inhabitants, the petitioners, is looked upon to be irregular and in*
> *defiance of the good and wholesome laws of the land and to be detest-*
> *able and [against] all good order.*[12]

The petitioners were William Williams, David Bush, Eli Root, J. Brown, and Woodbridge Little, but the petition was written by Little.[13] He was a Pittsfield attorney and a Tory. His condemnation of the Boston Tea Party might be understood in that light. However, on January 19, 1774, the town met and voted to support his view. While supporting the petition at the town meeting, the inhabitants of Pittsfield also wanted it known: "At the same time we are as averse as any of the patriots in America to being subjected to a tax without our own free and voluntary consent."[14]

The story of Woodbridge Little illustrates many things; not the least is how women became so involved. During the War for Independence, from the Boston Tea Party to victory, Woodbridge Little strategized, fought at times, fled at times, and capitulated in order to prevail. His enemy was not the British but his fellow citizens in Pittsfield. This is the lesser-told story of the Revolutionary War. In order to understand it, set aside the Hollywood version: The Revolutionary War did not begin as an enthusiastic call to arms to which all rallied without fear or ambivalence.

If they were "as averse as any patriot" to taxation without representation, why did they condemn the Boston Tea Party? Early on, many colonists, both Tories and Whigs, did not envision a war or an independent nation. They foresaw a negotiation with the Crown leading to better terms and conditions for the colonies: violence and destruction of property were unlikely to lead to the desired reasonable discourse.

Furthermore, Pittsfield was keeping a close eye on its purse. They wanted it made very clear that they judged the Boston Tea Party "unjustifiable conduct not duly authorized." Otherwise they feared "the owners of said tea will doubtless seek compensation [and we] as inhabitants may be obliged to pay them large sums."

Little had been smart. While condemning the Boston Tea Party, he had supported opposition to taxation and appealed to those fearing a suit for damages. In 1774 that was enough for Little to garner the support of the town. That would change. In the months from January to December 1774 there were imposed a series of "intolerable acts." The Americans no longer believed in peaceful resolution with the Crown, and war was declared. Tories in America, like Little, became enemies of the states. Initially Tories fled to avoid imprisonment.

Whereas Major Israel Stoddard and Woodbridge Little, Esq., both of Pittsfield, in the county of Berkshire, have fled from their respective homes, and are justly esteemed the common pests of society, and the incurable enemies of their country, and are supposed to be somewhere in New York government, moving sedition and rebellion against their country, it is hereby recommended to all friends of American liberty, and to all who do not delight in the innocent blood of their countrymen, to exert themselves that they may be taken into custody

and committed to some of His Majesty's jails until the civil war,
which has broken out in this province, may be ended.[15]

Unfortunately, because Little fled, his property was forfeited. It could be seized and given to Patriots. If he returned, he would be imprisoned; if he stayed away, he would be impoverished. Little found a middle ground. He arranged to return and swear allegiance to the cause. "Woodbridge Little, Israel Stoddard, Moses Graves, J. Hobby, J. Weston, and Joseph Clark made their appearance before the town and upon their confession, declaration, and taking of oath to the United Independent States of America, were received as the friends of these States."

Little dodged the bullet, kept his mouth shut, and was received into the life of Pittsfield. The process of forgiveness by the town followed closely the process for forgiveness and reinstatement into the Congregational Church: confession, sincere repentance, and re-acceptance into the religious community. Was Little's conversion sincere? There was some indication that he remained in communication with Tories in New York, and he was opposed to Allen and his Constitutionalists. On the other hand Little lived in peace in Pittsfield until his death.

Your neighbor could be allied with the enemy. A professed patriot might be a Tory, a Royalist, and a spy. It may have created tension and suspicion, but it also facilitated a woman being a spy.

A Woman's Place

From her vantage point . . .
—NATIONAL WOMEN'S HISTORY MUSEUM

If a woman's place was in the home, it did not interfere with Lydia Darragh's being a spy. Lydia Barrington was born in Ireland in 1728. She married William Darragh in 1753. Quakers, they soon immigrated to the colonies. They settled in Philadelphia, where William worked as a tutor and Lydia as a midwife.

The British marched into Philadelphia triumphant in 1777. General Sir William Howe defeated Washington, drove him from the city.

Washington retreated to Whitemarsh, Maryland (ninety miles distant), and Howe set up his headquarters directly across the street from the Darragh house.

Many evacuated the city, leaving only those who were Royalists and those who were accepted as neutral in the conflict. In that latter group were the Quakers. Their neutrality was accepted and therefore they were safe living among the British troops.

Lydia began her work as a spy immediately. "From her vantage point as a neighbor Lydia spied for General Washington's army . . . with her fourteen year old son as messenger."[16]

On December 2, 1777, Darragh was told her house would be used for a meeting that night. She and her family were to leave. Lydia sent her youngest children away, but begged to stay herself. That night she crept from her bedroom, hid in an adjacent cupboard, and listened to the meeting. What she heard chilled her. In two days, on December 4, they were planning a surprise attack on Washington at Whitemarsh.

It was now December 3, 1777: How was she to warn General Washington? The distance to Whitemarsh was great, and she feared for her young son's safety if he were to go. She believed a woman would raise less suspicion than a man so she did not tell her husband. She decided to go herself.

Here the story has more than one version. In one Lydia reaches Washington and delivers the news. In another she goes to the Rising Sun Tavern, a place notorious as a message center, and finds a soldier whom she entrusts to deliver the message. In a third she meets a rebel officer on the road and he carries the message the rest of the way.

Regardless of the details, through her efforts, Washington was warned and Howe's surprise attack failed.

In her daughter Ann's version there is a tantalizing postscript. Howe knew someone had warned Washington and that he was therefore prepared. Howe sent Major John Andre, reputedly a master spy and the man who recruited Benedict Arnold, to question people. Andre questioned Lydia, and the mild Quaker housewife outsmarted the master spy, who left satisfied that she had nothing to do with communicating Howe's plans to Washington.

What of Lydia? She was condemned by the Quakers, as was Betsy Ross for siding in a war. She survived the war, was first feted, then doubted, and finally believed.

Myths and Legends

The women's stories endured even when they were questioned. Most of the stories of female daring-do are true; some are not.

Somehow Abigail Adams's famous letter to her husband ("Remember the ladies . . .") was used as an example of the first plea for a woman's right to vote. That is probably not true. It was more likely a plea for an end to feme covert. Molly Pitcher was not a real person but a symbol representative of the many women who carried pitchers of water to cool the cannons so soldiers could reload and fire them again. From the hot lead they poured into bullet molds to the pitchers of water that cooled the cannons, women were there on the fields of battle.

At Fort Washington near Charleston in 1776, John Corbin stood on his post as an assistant gunner. When the fort came under attack, the senior gunner was soon dead. John took over and his wife Margaret stood his post cooling the cannon with water, a "Molly Pitcher," and helping her husband load. When he fell dead, she alone loaded and fired until she was hit.

Like Lydia Darragh, Betsy Ross was a Quaker but "not a humble seamstress; she was a skilled upholsterer with a thriving business and while she may have sewn a flag, there is little proof of it."[17] However, Betsy Ross may have done something much more important.

The Mistresses

It was the fall of 1776 and Washington, chased out of New York, was waiting his chance to cross the Delaware into Philadelphia. The British were relying on the Hessian soldiers under the command of Col. Carl Von Donrop to march to their aid in Trenton. Von Donrop did not come.

In his diary he wrote he would stay in Mount Holly because of an "exceedingly beautiful young widow."[18] Donrop stayed with the widow over Christmas, and Washington crossed the Delaware unmolested.

No one knows for certain who the widow was or whether she knew the significance of keeping the Hessian soldiers in Mount Holly. Some believe it was Betsy Ross. Their proof is circumstantial.

Ross was reported to be "a blue-eyed beauty."[19] She was condemned by the Quakers: "and she does not appear to condemn or repent her breach."[20] What was her breach: marriage to John Ross, an Episcopalian, or too much involvement in a war? Betsy was widowed in January 1776. She had relatives in Mount Holly, and may have spent Christmas with them. Finally she met Washington the previous year and may have been recruited as a spy then. However, a contemporary account states the fair madam was the widow of a doctor, which John Ross was not. Ross was apprentice to an upholsterer before the war and then a soldier.

Whoever the widow was, she did an excellent job to the benefit of General Washington and is remembered as the "mysterious widow of Mount Holly."

It was 1813, and the man who earlier wrote "We hold these truths to be self evident that all men are created equal" changed his mind. In the correspondence between the two former presidents, Thomas Jefferson told John Adams there was a "natural aristocracy among men." This natural aristocracy was based upon a man's superior virtue and talents.

Adams agreed but went further. What of female aristocrats, he asked. Women can be as formidable as the males. "What chance talents and virtue in competition with wealth, birth, and beauty? Any one of them can overbear either or both of the other two," Adams concluded.

Jefferson never replied. A pity: That exchange could have been interesting.

Just when you were prepared to accept that eighteenth-century colonial women were colorless, nameless, illiterate, industrious but boring, people who served alternately as plow horses and brood mares, Adams implies he knows women who are anything but. There were beautiful and seductive women whose dalliances affected the outcome of the Revolutionary War whether they intended them to or not.

Joshua Loring Jr. was one of our own—a Massachusetts boy. He was the son of General Joshua Loring. He married the beautiful blond Elizabeth, and served in Suffolk County as High Sheriff. When war came, his father said, "I have always eaten the king's bread and always will." He fled for England. Joshua Jr. carved out a different path.

At a party in Boston Joshua and Elizabeth were introduced to General William Howe, the man chosen by King George to lead the British troops against the rebels in the colonies. The three stepped from that Boston dinner table into the pages of history.

Reputedly, Elizabeth Loring and the general became lovers. Joshua was a cuckold but complicit. When the general moved his troops to New York, Joshua was given the post of Commissioner of Prisoners in New York. He was well compensated, but it is unclear exactly what his responsibilities were—unclear to us today and evidently to him then. He was later held responsible for the death of thousands of prisoners from disease and starvation.

Mrs. Loring entertained the general so thoroughly that New York was lost, although the British troops were better armed, better fed, better clothed, and more numerous. Condemning the lady for her unintentional assistance to the rebels, Sir Francis Hopkinson wrote "The Battle of the Kegs."

Sir William he, snug as a flea,
Lay all the time a snoring,
Nor dreamed of harm
As he lay warm
In bed with Mrs. Loring.[21]

In eighteenth-century America, premarital sex was granted a wink and a nod, but adultery was a sin. Was Mrs. Loring a sinner? When the general went to Philadelphia, Elizabeth accompanied him while her husband continued abusing and neglecting prisoners in New York. In Philadelphia she did serve as the general's hostess; however, the only accusers of the lady were two very angry loyalists: Hopkinson and Judge Thomas Jones.

In his history of New York written a decade after the war ended, Jones wrote: "As Cleopatra of old lost Mark Anthony the world, so did this illustrious courtesan lose Sir William Howe the honor, the laurels, and the glory of putting an end to one of the most obstinate rebellions that ever existed."[22]

Well, well, did she or didn't she? Did she mean to or not? We do not know any more than we know the name of the widow of Mount Holly.

These women were not colorless, nameless, or boring. All support Adams's contention and dispute the idea that some "notable women" of the eighteenth century were unworthy of note; they were remarkable.

The Wives

It was 1777 and Margaret Shipton was an acknowledged beauty. She was also merry, sociable, a creature of fashion, and seventeen years old. Philadelphia was in the hands of the British, and Margaret (Peggy to her friends) was a Tory, at least for the nonce. Benedict Arnold was none of these things. Crippled and embittered by war, and what he deemed "slights" by his superiors, Arnold was still a patriot, well weathered if not well worn.

All Peggy's youth and beauty was a heady mix for the British officers and evidently also for Peggy. She was subject to fits. Occasionally she was overcome with paroxysms, spasms accompanied by outbursts of laughter and babble. Whatever the cause, extent, or cure, these fits did not interfere with her popularity or fun. She especially enjoyed the attentions of a British officer named John Andre, handsome, sophisticated, and insinuating. General Howe's spy, Andre had recently questioned Lydia Darragh, so however clever he might be, he was not invincible.

In war fortunes change. General Washington recaptured Philadelphia, and Arnold marched in as commander of the city in 1778. Arnold and Peggy met. They were married the following year.

There is no mystery about what happened. John Andre was captured by the patriots. He was carrying papers that proved Arnold had conspired to help the British take West Point—a key strategic position. Andre was hung as a spy. Arnold was condemned as a traitor and escaped to England. Peggy, now mother of the first of five children she would bear Arnold, followed.

Here is the only mystery: Who was Peggy Shipton Arnold—instigator, co-conspirator, or innocent young wife?

Washington, Hamilton, and Richard Varrick all interviewed her and were satisfied with her innocence. Varrick wrote that after questioning her, he "ran up the stairs and there met the miserable lady raving distracted."[23]

Her fits served her well; whenever questioned or accused, she had one. She was released and joined her husband in England. She was loved in England as a true Tory, and forgiven in America as an innocent betrayed in love. Only Aaron Burr, that consummate lady's man, remained certain she was complicit.

The Dispatchers

Paul Revere was not the only rider. Many more than one rode through the night with important messages, and some were women.

There was a twenty-year-old Connecticut woman, Deborah Champion, who rode into the pages of history by default. Her father was Col. Henry Champion. When a rider came with an important message to be relayed to General Washington, it was clear he was too exhausted to go on. The colonel asked his own daughter to carry the message. Deborah was swift but she was also clever. Early in the morning, she was stopped by a sentry. She talked her way out of being taken to his superior. She convinced the soldier he would be reprimanded for waking an officer. He was uncertain and Deborah rode on. She made it through and was thanked by Washington himself for her courage and patriotism.[24]

A sixteen-year-old girl named Sybil Ludington rode the back roads of Putnam, New York. She was also a colonel's daughter. He had word that there was an attack in Danbury, Connecticut, and the New York militia was needed to swell the ranks. Sybil rode, knocking on farmhouse doors, rousing militiamen, and, it is said, saving the day at Danbury. The British destroyed the arms depot and were overrunning General Benedict Arnold's troops when the New York contingent arrived. They were called "Ludington Troops," and the young lady's namesakes turned the tide.

Often these women benefitted from those who underestimated or even denigrated women; Emily Geiger did. She volunteered to ride between Generals Nathaniel Greene and Charles Sumter. Riding side saddle, she rested at a farm owned by Royalists. When British riders arrived and questioned the farmer, he told them of his guest. The British correctly surmised that she was a dispatch rider for the rebels, but they incorrectly concluded she would be easy to capture. They meant to rest first. While they did, Emily escaped and made it to Sumter's camp. Greene's plan for a joint attack upon the British was safely delivered.

Dressed as Men

Margaret Corbin donned men's clothing to stand beside her husband on the battlements and was congratulated. Ann Bailey was fined and jailed for attempting to enlist when dressed as a man, and so was Ann Smith. What was the difference? The women fined, or worse, "drummed through the town," as prostitutes would be, were discovered when they tried to enlist. There was an 80 pound bounty paid for enlisting, and a woman attempting to collect it was considered a fraud.

Deborah Samson[25] was more successful. It was 1778 in Plympton, Massachusetts, that Samson enlisted as a young man named Robert Shirtliffe. He was accepted and assigned to the company of Captain Nathan Thayer. Dressed as a man, Deborah served as Shirtliffe for three years. The story of her life as a soldier is extraordinary precisely because it was so normal. She served without incident and fought bravely. She went undiscovered even after being treated for wounds. When wounded a second time, the doctor, Binney of Philadelphia, discovered her secret and kept it. He removed her from the camp to his house for treatment. However, when she recovered, the doctor met with Thayer. Thayer issued an order that Shirtliffe deliver a letter to General Washington.

In silence, the story goes, General Washington handed her discharge papers in the name of Shirtliffe and an amount of money for her passage home. Deborah married, and after the war Mrs. Benjamin Gannet received an invitation from Washington. When they met he thanked her for her service. This is one of no fewer than four versions of this story, but all agree on the central point: A young girl from Massachusetts fought bravely in the American Revolution while dressed as a man.

The Martin sisters[26] were at home in South Carolina when they heard of a dispatch being carried to a British general. The contents were of so important a nature that the courier was accompanied by two guards. Their men were all away fighting the British, and the wives determined to do some good. They dressed in their husbands' clothes, took up arms, and went into the nearby woods to wait and waylay the British soldiers. Their mission was successful. They surprised the men, took their packet, and hurried home by way of a short-cut. This story is a fine example of courage and resource but is one among many, and may not have been remembered without the aftermath.

No sooner had they arrived home and changed into their own clothes than the same three British soldiers arrived at the Martins' front door. They said they were weary and had experienced a terrible misadventure on the road. May they enter and rest? The women were too curious, and perhaps of too teasing a nature, to deny them. They sat together and the soldiers told the women of the violent men who had accosted and overpowered them. Imagine with what difficulty the two sisters suppressed laughter and feigned sympathy.

Camp Followers

The camp followers to the British in the French and Indian War were said to be wives and servants who performed as cooks, laundresses, and nurses. When the army was well supplied, the camp follower's life was tolerable. As war dragged on, the band of camp followers became motlier. They were also mistresses and prostitutes, the displaced and the desperate straggling behind, living on less and less.

Despite the disdain heaped upon them by soldiers who called camp followers *human luggage*; despite the pejoratives like *trulls, doxies, jades,* and *strums*; despite the condemnation laced with pity heaped upon them by other women, "such a sordid set of creatures in human figure"[27]— camp followers performed needed tasks and sometimes heroic deeds. They took empty canteens and filled them, bringing them back to the men in the field of battle, slaking the thirst of the dying and those still able to fight. They picked up a musket and manned the cannon of a fallen soldier. They nursed the wounded where they lay on the field, and dragged and carried them out of harm's way when they were able. They cooked and fed, sewed and scrubbed, and they walked behind the army, forbidden ever to ride.

Other Battles

It is difficult enough to tell the stories of women who did not record their own; women who were illiterate or literate only to the point of signing their names and reading their Bibles—the text of which they may have long since committed to memory. It is doubly difficult when the woman has risen to the stature of legend. Then added to the other difficulties there is too much material, too many conflicting reports, and possibly due to the desire to embellish, too much that seems unlikely. The story of Mum Bett was such a tale.

Born into slavery circa 1742, Bett was the property of Pieter Hogeboom, a farmer in Claverack, New York. When his daughter Hannah married John Ashley of Sheffield, Massachusetts, he gave Bett to her to take to her new home. It may have been done with the same attitude that Mr. Lane delivered a clock to each daughter, a father's contribution to the furnishings of his daughter's new household as part of her marital portion, a sign that Hogeboom had fulfilled his duty to his offspring without acknowledgment of Bett's humanity.

Here the story becomes less clear. The events move smoothly to the anticipated conclusion. There is a satisfying clarity about who the good guys and bad guys are. There just isn't any proof, no substantiation.

Nonetheless here is the story: Mum Bett, now the mother of a young girl (hence the title Mum), is hit with a hot poker by an angry, unkind, and unreasonable Hannah. In another version, Mum Bett's daughter Betsy is about to be hit by the aforesaid mean Hannah, and the mother steps between. In a third version Bett's younger sister, slow if not retarded, tries the patience of Hannah and she is about to be hit. The version is in dispute, the result is not: Bett is hit in the upper arm.

Mum Bett is scarred for life and wears a bandage in the hope that people will ask what happened and she can reply, "Ask Madam." Thus Mum Bett would establish her moral superiority and innate supremacy. Therefore she asks: "Now who is slave and who master?"

It's a good story, but the problem is that the record of it is retold in a fictional story by Catharine Sedgwick written many years after the events. Both the genre and the elapsed time relieve Catharine of the necessity to adhere to a strict rendition.

Similarly, Catharine wrote that Mum Bett said if she could have one minute of freedom even if the price was that she would die in the next minute, she would take it so she might stand on the earth one moment a free woman. Perhaps she said that; perhaps that is how she felt; or perhaps Catharine put those words in her mouth.

Here is what we do know: In 1781, in the midst of the Revolutionary War, Mum Bett fought a battle of her own. She sued for her freedom and won. Illiterate, Mum Bett could not read the burgeoning literature about human rights and freedom, but she could listen. As she apparently told Theodore Sedgwick, she learned by "keeping still and minding things."

She listened to the table talk at Colonel Ashley's house and to recitations in the village square. The next question is: To what was Mum Bett listening? There are also different ideas about what exactly Bett heard: the US Constitution, the Constitution of the Commonwealth of Massachusetts, or the Sheffield Resolves?

On January 5, 1773, eleven men met in an upstairs room of Col. John Ashley's house in Sheffield. Together they wrote a declaration against British tyranny and for the rights of the people of the colonies. It was sent to the town meeting on January 12 for approval. Once approved, the Sheffield Resolves were published in the *Massachusetts Spy* (also known as *Thomas' Boston Journal*).

The resolves open: "Mankind in a state of nature are equal, free, and independent, and have a right to the undisturbed enjoyment of their lives, their liberty, and their property." There are ten "resolves," including no taxation without representation, the right to a trial, and equality under the law.[28]

Bett was in the household when the resolves were written by Ashley, Sedgwick, and other Sheffield gentlemen. Bett may have heard the language then. It was also an opportunity for her to meet or at least know who Theodore Sedgwick was. Two things oppose this version. First, would Bett have waited seven years after she heard the words to act?

Furthermore, Sedgwick would have been forced to tell her that while laudable the resolves did not change the law.

Was it 1780 when she heard the words that would free her? In 1780 Allen and the Constitutionalists finally won their point. A new Massachusetts Constitution was written. Prior to ratification, it was circulated and read in town and village squares.

The words she heard would have been these: "All men are born free and equal and have certain natural, essential, and unalienable rights." According to legend, Mum Bett believed those lines could set her free.

In either version she then walks to the Sheffield home of Theodore Sedgwick to ask the meaning of the words. He explains. Hearing that those words could mean an end to slavery in Massachusetts, she asks him to take her case. He agrees.

In another version, Ashley and Sedgwick, friends and political allies, plan to bring a case to establish a precedent that will put an end to slavery in Massachusetts. They explain the plan to both Bett and a male slave named Brom; they ask the two to go forward with the case. They agree.

Regardless of which specifics led to the day, in August 1781 the case of *Brom and Bett v. Ashley* was heard in court. Brom and Bett won.

It is interesting that Ashley, though well represented, through his attorneys, merely states the underlying argument for slavery: One man has the legal right to own another; when owned, the slave is legally his servant for life. When Ashley loses, he has created a clear record, therefore, of what is defeated. There is precedent that one human being cannot and does not own another under the Constitution of Massachusetts. While Ashley files an appeal, he immediately withdraws it. Ashley then offers Bett her job back for wages; she declines, and accepts employment in the Sedgwick household.

It is not the first "freedom case" in Massachusetts as sometimes reported. It is the second; the first is brought by Quark Walker. However, Bett is the first woman to be freed in Massachusetts under the new constitution. When there is an appeal in the Walker case, the *Brom/Bett* decision is cited as precedent and Walker wins his appeal.

With her move to the Sedgwick house on the plain in Stockbridge, Mum Bett asks Sedgwick for a final legal service: She changes her name from the one given her by an owner to one she gives herself. Mum Bett is henceforward Elizabeth Freeman. Regardless of the dispute over details, the story is worth telling, the victory worth remembering.

Elizabeth Freeman's life and exceptional experiences bridge the wars. She fought her own battle in court during the Revolutionary War, and would fight men to a standoff during Shays' Rebellion. Whether true or apocryphal, her stories are worth telling because she is well worth remembering—not because of those things she may or may not have done, but in the end for those things we know she did. She was the mainstay of the Sedgwick household. When Pamela Sedgwick's woes, so sympathetically referred to by Mary Bidwell, left Pamela helpless, Elizabeth Freeman was truly the notable woman and little mother in the Sedgwick house.

When she left the Sedgwick household, she became a property owner, a sought-after midwife, and respected member of the Stockbridge community. The text on her tombstone, also written by Catharine, is witness to a great woman, her legacy etched in stone:

> *Elizabeth Freeman known by the name Mumbet*
> *Died December 28, 1829. Her supposed age was 85 years.*
> *She was born a slave and remained a slave for nearly thirty years.*
> *She could neither read nor write and yet in her own sphere she had*
> *no superior or equal. She neither wasted time nor property.*
> *She never violated a trust nor failed to perform a duty.*
> *In every situation of domestic trial, she was the most efficient helper*
> *and the tenderest friend. Good Mother, farewell.*[29]

Shays' Rebellion

In 1787 as the Constitution of the United States was being written,[30] Shays' Rebellion was squelched on a field in Sheffield, Massachusetts. Shays' men were called the "Regulators" because they wanted to regulate laws that disproportionately favored the wealthy. They wanted to give more protection to the poor. Shays and his men were also called traitors and murderers. They were tried and sentenced to prison and to hang.

George Washington dismissed Daniel Shays as irrelevant, but James Madison said Shays exposed weaknesses, excesses, and injustices that had to be addressed in order to have a strong republic. The battle was couched in eighteenth-century terms: the merchant class versus the farmers.

Daniel Shays closed the courts and freed prisoners to stop "debt" trials wherein farms were dispossessed and debtors imprisoned. They were rebelling against taxes levied to pay Revolutionary War debt.

In 1786, after the Revolutionary War, the country was heavily in debt. To reduce the debt, taxes were imposed. It was generally felt that the heaviest tax burden fell on the poorest citizens. The poor, primarily farmers, were already reeling from personal debt. The amount of personal debt was exacerbated by their Revolutionary War service, which took them away from their farms. As profits fell, mortgages increased. Though promised compensation for military service, they were paid in worthless currency that even the government would not accept in payment of taxes ("not worth a continental"). The combination of these economic pressures created "desperate debtors." They were the ones who could not pay and faced dispossession of all they owned. These debtors were hauled into court; there, harsh laws favored the lenders not the debtors, and they left court penniless and in chains.

This already bad situation was made worse because there was an obvious disparity in wealth between lenders and borrowers that created class warfare between the merchants and the farmer, the gentlemen and the yeomen.

The *Hartford Courant* called the farmers and those in debt "the most discontentedest." Though not a word (then or now), the superlative accurately described them, and it was they who became the soldiers in Shays' Rebellion.

The call for help was unheard, so Shays and his men rebelled. During 1786–1787 as Shays' ranks swelled with farmers and laborers, as the skirmishes multiplied, there were those who feared it would grow into a civil war. There is something about war at the doorstep that involves the women more readily; some may cower in fear but most acted decisively and some even saved their men.

February 1787 was Shays' last stand. He was not with them when his army marched from the New York border through Stockbridge,

Old house on Plain Street, Stockbridge
JOHN WARNER BARBER, *HISTORICAL COLLECTIONS*, 1841, P. 98

Massachusetts, to Great Barrington and finally to that fateful field in Sheffield on the Connecticut border. They took prisoners along the way, beat and pillaged. It was a harrowing night.

At the Woodbridge house in Stockbridge, the inmates woke to a room full of Shays' Regulators. Boy and man were transfixed, and were marched out into the snow without resistance. At Deacon Ingersoll's the scene would have repeated but his good wife remembered an unopened bottle of brandy and negotiated a trade. Shays' men left with the brandy and without the deacon.

At Sedgwick house, the army was confronted by a single aging black woman. Elizabeth Freeman stood silently by as they threw out the window Sedgwick's "ruffled shirts and parlor costumes . . . the appurtenances of gentility."[31] She then went to her room and sat on the trunk at the foot of her bed while they searched the house for someone to kidnap and for treasure to carry away.

Empty handed they returned to Elizabeth's room where she remained atop the chest unmoved and unmoving. They demanded silver and gold. She said there was none. They insisted on searching her room. "You call me a poor nigger yet you stoop to robbing me."[32]

Chastened, the men left. Once the house was free of intruders, Freemen rose from the chest where she had hidden all the Sedgwick valuables.

Miss Mercy Scott, the village seamstress, was robbed of her silver shoe buckles—nothing less and nothing more.

On Plain Street they entered Widow Bingham's tavern with their thirty-two prisoners. Laden with arms and plunder, they declared the tavern "headquarters."[33] There is no firm record, but village lore has Anna hiding those she could in cupboards in the tavern to save them from the rebels, and plying the rebels with liquor until they passed out or could no longer stand. The rest went out into the night bound for Great Barrington where the losses were not as clear to determine.

The government's plan was to stop the rebellion at Sheffield. Volunteers were to meet with General Fellows's militia in Sheffield. Though they knew the line of the rebels' march, the men left their women in Great Barrington unprotected, and went south into Sheffield.

The men instructed their wives not to resist or fight or to make the rebels angry. Amazing—a mob of angry men drunk with liquor and power, a mob that already broke the law and that knew there would be consequences, entered the town and the private homes of the citizens, the men left, the women were abandoned and were told not to resist.

There is no record of a single rape, murder, or act of violence against a woman. That is, in the subsequent court proceedings there are no such charges brought.

There is no record of what the women did to effect this outcome except that many gathered together in one house. Perhaps the vulnerability of one woman was mitigated by numbers. Perhaps they gave their intruders food and drink as Anna Bingham and Mrs. Ingersoll did. Perhaps they gave up their silver adornments as Mercy Scott did. Perhaps they sat firm and shamed the men as Elizabeth Freeman did. Whatever they did, they survived the night. Perhaps they simply did not report what happened; perhaps no official inquired.

The rebels lost to General Fellows; they were tried and most were hanged. Were they as bad as the eighteenth-century courts found or as good as Madison thought?

The comfort of history is not that it gets it right every time in real time. Those who say history is written by the victors make a solid point. The comfort of history is that when time cools the heat of the moment, when the very vocal self-server is dead, and yesterday's special interest is irrelevant tomorrow, history corrects itself and reports the facts. With time there is truth and justice usually, but sometimes two versions of historic events stand without hope of resolution.

Among the never-to-be-resolved conflicts are these: What is the relevance of the Sheffield Resolutions, and who was Daniel Shays?

History eventually chooses between versions but not in those two cases. Wise historians say of the resolutions: Read them and decide for yourself what Jefferson owed to the men of Sheffield. In the case of Daniel Shays, history fails utterly. His place in history, even his character, is never immutable. Whether he is Washington's irrelevant side show, Madison's key figure in the shape of the new republic, or General Fellows's terrorist, how he is viewed continually changes. How he is viewed in each decade is a reflection of the politics of the day without any permanent conclusion.

The women, however, are remembered with respect as courageous and resourceful under fire. With Bett and Chamberlain, it is for what they did; for the women of Great Barrington, perhaps, it is for what they did not do.

Part Two

Post War and the New Century

Chapter 8

Revolution in Women's Lives and Roles

A time line of legal rights and protections for women:[1]

right to own property (1809); the age of consent raised from ten to sixteen years (1886); rape a violent crime (1898); right to vote (1920); control over her own body (abortion and contraception, 1973); ability to borrow money without a male cosigner/have a credit card (1974); the right to serve in the military (enlist in, 1917; accepted as member of, 1948; attend military academy, 1978); right to keep job if pregnant (1978); beating wife a violent crime (—); equal pay for equal work (—).

In a new country on the threshold of a new century, what could women expect? In going to war, authority was defied; in fighting the war, traditional roles were challenged; in winning the war, a government was toppled. As a new form of government emerged, it is fair to ask, did the Revolutionary War change women's lives? The short form of the answer is: not much. The laws remained the same and the hierarchy held. And yet . . .

Seeds were planted and the characteristics of ideal womanhood started to change. The changes were incremental, as much a change of heart as a change in the law. The notable woman—obedient, industrious, fruitful, and frugal—was being replaced by the darling of the drawing room—still obedient but also pretty, well mannered, and charming. As the nineteenth century progressed, as the country became wealthier, the middle class grew, and as more moved to the cities, a majority of people would imitate the ways of the drawing room. The upper class, not the saints, would provide the role models. The wife as companion would gain ground on the goodwife.

Hannah Dustin

> *[W]ould that the bloody old hag had been drowned.*
> —Nathaniel Hawthorne

Early nineteenth-century writers searched the eighteenth century for examples of pioneer strength, perseverance, and triumph. Hannah Dustin was not overlooked but she was no longer accepted without demur.

Timothy Dwight questioned her actions. In 1821, in his *Travels in New England and New York,* Dwight wanted to know if Hannah's suffering before the night of the killings, or even her anticipation of future suffering, justified the slaughter. He was appalled by the scalping and murder for bounty.[2]

Henry David Thoreau withheld overt criticism but equally withheld praise. Nathaniel Hawthorne was not subtle. In an article Hawthorne admired Thomas Dustin, but wrote of Hannah: "[W]ould that the bloody old hag had been drowned."[3]

Even after Hawthorne acknowledged the two most disturbing details, that her infant child was killed before her eyes and that her husband did more to protect the children than her, Hawthorne had no sympathy for Hannah. He condemned her violence, and he was critical of Cotton Mather for praising her.

In the eighteenth century Mather wanted heroes and heroines and found Hannah. Dwight, Thoreau, and Hawthorne wanted heroes and heroines, but it was the nineteenth century, and the definition of a good woman had changed.

No longer a heroine, no longer a heroic tale, Hannah's story raised more questions than it answered. Is killing ever justified? Is seeking pecuniary reward for violent acts ever moral? Are the standards different for men and women? On what basis, if any, is Hannah to be admired?[4] In the new republic the answers to those questions had changed.

The goodwife was a sturdy chief of production, capable of carrying a gun. The good woman of the nineteenth century was feminine, and by definition femininity was without aggression. The goody was materialistic because it was practical to be so and in the best interests of her husband and family. The new woman for a new century in a new country was not materialistic because it was indelicate and worse, could be construed as competitive with men. The goodwife demanded sexual gratification. Her sexual desires had to be regulated within the bounds of marriage. Her granddaughter's sexuality need not be regulated because it was almost nonexistent. The sexual appetites natural in men were reputedly absent in a good woman. Both women were obedient, but the nineteenth-century wife was obedient out of love not duty.

These ideas and characteristics were changing because the underpinnings that held women in place were changing: the very concept of God, the impregnable position of the Church, and the basis for marriage.

God of Vengeance, God of Love

God as He is presently composed . . .[5]

By the start of the nineteenth century many of the Puritan dogmas—predestination, infant damnation and the total depravity of man—had been rejected and replaced by a God of Love.[6]

Soon this new religious concept, this new composition of God, led to a new idea. If life was not predestined, it could be shaped, changed, and improved by human exertion. Moreover it should be. As God was redefined, so America was renamed. It was Arcadia, the "New Eden." Americans were inspired to improve.

These new religious beliefs led to the creation of reform societies. The societies were formed, if not to create heaven on earth, to strive for it.

Orphanages were built. There were societies for improved education, improved conditions for prisoners, humane treatment of the mentally and physically impaired. There were societies against drinking, against capital punishment and slavery.

These reform societies, initiated in the churches, had an unintended consequence. Women were handed a role, a purpose outside the home. The tasks fell within the woman's social circle. Her role was broadened geographically because it was unchanged from a role she had always played in succoring the poor, tending and comforting the sick, and educating the very young.

Furthermore one reform movement, one that captured the imagination of the nation, was in the hands of women. The fight for abolition was not quite the same as the fight against slavery. Many who were morally opposed to slavery feared a constitutional amendment abolishing slavery. They believed abolition would lead to the dissolution of the union. They did not doubt that the former was an evil practice but believed the latter was an evil outcome.

On both sides of that issue were female spokespeople. Catharine Sedgwick was very concerned for the cohesion of the union, and of course, her concern would prove true. However, her friend Harriet Beecher Stowe replied, if there were no other way to abolish slavery then "the Union will have to give way."

Some leaders who hotly pursued abolition became famous and garnered respect. Harriet Beecher Stowe was not just nationally but internationally famous after publication of *Uncle Tom's Cabin*. Abolition challenged the limits of a woman's role and abilities just as the Revolutionary War did. Hannah Dustin, Deborah Samson, the Martin sisters, Harriet Beecher Stowe, Catharine Sedgwick, and others were demonstrating and being rewarded for abilities beyond the norm.

The new spirit within the church, the creation of these other reform movements, also created a space and a vocabulary for the women's rights movement. That does not mean that the power structure was toppling. This was not a time when women were power brokers or those who shaped what was; they were not central figures at all. What happened around them defined them as surely as anything they could do individually.

The Change in the Church

. . . receiving Mrs. Austin to their communion while under censure . . . [7]

They left England to worship as they pleased, and now they did not seem to know how they were pleased to worship. The sermons of the Reverend West were two hours long and accepted as the word of God. Slowly people wondered, albeit silently, which was worse, the length or the presumption.

The absolute power and impregnable position of the Congregational Church suffered its first challenge as early as 1742 when a legal exception to the town tax that supported the Congregational minister was granted to members of the Church of England in Sheffield, Massachusetts.[8]

The Supreme Court decision in 1792 had a broader reach. All residents were taxed for the support of the Congregational Church and the minister's salary. In addition, in many villages, all citizens regardless of religious affiliation were required to attend the Congregational Church at least once in three months. Accordingly they were assigned and charged for a pew. The case brought objected on the grounds that it was in conflict with the freedom of worship granted by the Constitution. Laughed out of state and local courts in theocratic Massachusetts, the case was won in the US Supreme Court.

These legal actions followed, rather than led, public opinion. There were chinks in the armor of the church long before there were laws challenging it. What those chinks were and how the power structure changed as a result are key to understanding the change in women's lives.

The Fisks and the Great Awakening

. . . the first known police officer killed in the line of duty in King Township . . . end of watch October 7, 1804[9]

The population in New England was growing, and as it grew it was somewhat more relaxed and more diversified. In New England, it was reported that there were more taverns than churches, and that attendance at the taverns was more religious. It was a report made with a scowl of disapproval by some and a chortle of glee by others.

In Great Barrington, Massachusetts, the Reverend Samuel Hopkins wrote: "The revival that has come down on many of the New England churches like showers that water the earth appears to have passed by

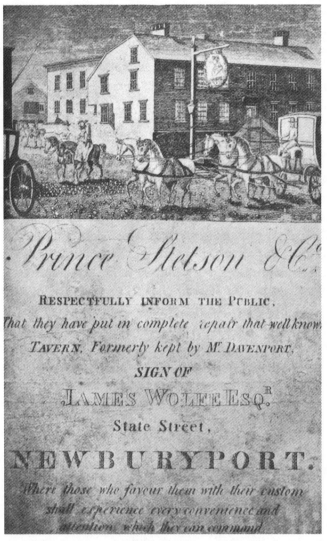

An advertisement for Wolfe's Tavern, Newburyport

ALICE MORSE EARLE, *HOME LIFE IN COLONIAL DAYS*, 1898, P. 538

Great Barrington." Hopkins reported experiencing "trials and discouragement, darkness and despondency." In 1748 in anticipation of joy and perhaps in capitulation, the reverend married Joanna, daughter of Moses Ingersoll, the first tavern owner in Great Barrington.

Hopkins's marriage was more successful than his efforts to guide his flock in the ways of the Great Awakening. They were uninterested and he was eventually fired. The Church's hold on lives in New England was no longer absolute. The bounds that held women in place, that justified her inferior position, were loosening. The revival, or "Great Awakening," was the very doctrine that had hobbled John Fisk in his effort to wed the Widow Deane.

Under its rule, Lavinia Deane Fisk was excommunicated. She lost her attempts to be reinstated, and was neither married in her church nor was her first child with Fisk baptized in Stockbridge. Moreover out of communion in one Congregational church, no other would accept her and the couple's first move was out of New England into Columbia County, New York.

Barely ten years later, October 27, 1788, the Congregational Church in New Haven, Connecticut, accepted a new member who had been excommunicated in Great Barrington. What was the consequence? None—everyone found an amicable way to forgive everyone else. The churches remained on friendly terms and Mrs. Austin remained in communion in New Haven.

Fortunately the story of John Fisk does not end on the road out of Stockbridge with his saddened and chastened wife. Their story goes on and they serve as examples of the changes that took place after the Revolutionary War. Their marriage survived the hardships and together they had six children. All six were baptized in a Congregational church and like Mrs. Austin no one cared that Lavinia had been excommunicated in Stockbridge.

They settled first in Grand Isle, Lake Champlain, Vermont, and eventually in King Township, Ontario, Canada. Once again Lavinia lived on a large farm with her children around her. Once again Fisk was singled out for service, respected and reelected as High Constable of the Home District. Once again he was entrusted with the transport of prisoners.

On October 7, 1804, twenty-seven years after Lavinia defied the church and married John, Fisk had charge of one prisoner en route to trial in New Castle. On stormy waters, the schooner HMCS *Speedy* capsized and sank. Fisk, his prisoner, and twenty others including the judge and prosecuting attorney, drowned. John Fisk's body was not recovered but a plaque was dedicated in his memory as "the first known police officer in King Township killed in the line of duty. [Fisk's] end of watch was October 7, 1804."

The Widow Deane, now the Widow Fisk, lived on. Excommunicated for ignoring an admonition of the church and consummating an unsanctioned marriage, Lavinia Higby Deane Fisk was indeed a poster child, but not for the Great Awakening as Reverend West hoped but for the weakening of the Congregational Church. It is doubtful that the Reverend West could have won his case at any subsequent time and doubtful that Reverend Allen would have brought it in the first place. Certainly Reverend Joseph Huntington, the minister representing the Fisks, would not have. He lived to see his notions about the nature of marriage and the right to sanction a marriage change as he argued.

Women and Love

Of all the elements in the gentle revolution to follow—working outside the home, keeping the wages and owning property, voting—the basis for marriage was the most revolutionary; it presaged the rest. Does it seem slight in comparison to the public gains? Without acknowledging the woman's right to choose a mate; without acknowledging her attractions and capabilities beyond laborer; without praising her for what she was not just what she could do, in short, without equality and equity in intimacy, there were no further possibilities.

As the hearthside became cheerier, the wives became more subdued. The sexual prudishness of which the eighteenth century is impugned was actually yet to come. Theirs was not a romp through the woods with Pan but a sober stroll through the Puritan pines; nonetheless, one might be surprised at the amount of "bump and tickle" there was in the eighteenth century. The sexual prudishness was actually a product of the next century.

The rules of etiquette, the rituals of courtship, customs, conventions, laws and prohibitions that guided and limited their choices became as rigid as any religious admonition. There was another twist. In the eighteenth century when it was assumed that both men and women had sexual appetites, the husband was the regulator of sexual conduct under his roof. He was responsible. With the new century, the new idea that women, good women, had less sexual appetite, she was responsible for her sexual behavior and her sexual misbehavior was considered aberrant.

The Etiquette of Wooing

The etiquette books were clear: felicity in marriage was the result of equality between the partners in cash and social currency. While church admonition was being replaced by etiquette books and a well-honed social prescription, the definition of a lady and a gentleman still had many of the elements of the definition of a good Christian.

To be a lady or gentleman was the goal of every right-thinking person. As the church loosened its grip, the etiquette book, sentimental novel, ballad, poem, and even the infamous bodice-ripper and blood-curdler took the place of catechism in directing behavior. The drive to read was for more than the reproofs of the Bible for the titillation of the novel. Literature was persuasive, and some young women were unduly excited by it.

The manners of society and the customs of courtship were neither arbitrary nor merely decorous but based upon the social principles and religious morals of the day. Puritanism was challenged but not entirely defeated. Now etiquette was meant to regulate.

Yet the road to matrimony was difficult for a woman to traverse. A lady could receive but not approach; she could accept but not invite. She was dependent upon a male family member to invite eligible gentlemen to the house, and the house formed the four corners of her world. She was locked in by custom.

Strictly speaking a lady was never alone with a man unless he was a relative, husband or fiancé. However, some young people found, through the contrivance of the family, that they were alone in the parlor or the garden for a short period. That was not an invitation for breaking the rules of conduct or conversation.

Conversation was the medium through which they took the measure of one another and decided if there was a future. While a gentleman was bounded by rules, a lady was simply bound. Through every conversation, she walked the thin line between good manners and flirtation. Manners required she be attentive, interested, sympathetic, but never coy, teasing, or frivolous. Delicacy and proper feeling required a gentleman to avoid certain subjects: sex, money, pregnancy, and crimes against persons—murder and rape. Gossip was permitted between members of the same sex but not members of the opposite sex. Any topic that might make the other uncomfortable was to be avoided. The cornerstone of good manners was respecting and attending to the comfort of others. With the rules firmly in mind, conversation began.

Through this somewhat restricted discourse, each sketched the character of the other. What they were trying to determine was the value of one another as a life partner. In the upper classes, each wanted a gentle mate. *Lady* and *gentleman* were not words used lightly: to be a lady or a gentleman was the goal of every right-thinking young person.

A lady paid attention to the comfort of others. She had good understanding and cool judgment. She was not to show emotion in public, or at least she was to properly regulate her emotions. In addition to cool judgment and regulated emotions, she was required to have strong feelings and an affectionate disposition. She was to be taught and have knowledge, talents, and skills, especially domestic skills, but never ever to be clever or to know more than a man.

A desire for too much knowledge was vanity, the same vanity that brought down Eden. It was desirable to be well disposed, but as everyone could not be pretty, it was mandatory that she be well turned out. Appropriate dress for every occasion was part of good behavior.

The gentleman had good understanding, knowledge of the world, taste, sense and goodness. He did not inflict pain but on the contrary eased the way for those around him. He was attentive without being intrusive, he was self-aware without being self-centered, and he never spoke about himself in public. His honor was of paramount importance. He did not act dishonorably toward a lady or in business.

Fortunately everyone understood these were paragons—ideals to be worked toward—and Christian forbearance demanded understanding and forgiveness of short-falls.

If his attentions to a lady were too steady and too intimate without purpose; if his attentions were therefore understood by her to form an engagement, honor might require him to marry her. However they reached the decision to marry, engagement required parental approval.

Commenting on the slender path American men and women walked, Gustave de Beaumont wrote in 1831,

> *Morals are extremely pure. A woman who does not conduct herself well is an extreme rarity. Unmarried men pay attention only to girls [single females]; these once married think only of their husbands. So long as they are not engaged, they [single females] exercise an extreme freedom in their relations.*

To Be or Not to Be . . . Married

This is a story that may surprise modern audiences. As early as 1810, Catharine Sedgwick chose a career over marriage. Her story shows the importance of marriage to the early nineteenth-century woman's economic well-being and social consequence and the concomitant difficulties in turning down a proposal of marriage. Her "young man" will be identified for the first time in print, and his story also told. Finally this section tells how Catharine defied convention; challenged ideas about the roles of men, women, and marriage; and helped to change those ideas.

In Stockbridge, in 1819, forty-four years after Lavinia Deane married for love and lost membership in the church, Catharine Sedgwick wrote her brother, "It is strange but it is impossible for me to create a sentiment of tenderness by any process of reasoning or any effort of gratitude." She was explaining her inability to love the man she had promised to marry. The choice seems clear to us. If you don't love him, don't marry him, but that decision was not as clear in 1819.

It would be forty more years before love was accepted as the best grounds for marriage. While church admonition was being replaced by etiquette books and a well-honed social prescription, the definition of a lady and a gentleman still had many of the elements of the definition of a good Christian.

Conversation and reputation were the mediums through which they took the measure of one another's character and decided if there was a future. Even if left alone for a short period, it was not an invitation to go beyond polite conversation.

In conversation, manners required she be attentive, interested, sympathetic, but never coy, teasing, or frivolous. Delicacy and proper feeling required men to avoid certain subjects: sex, money, pregnancy, and crime. Gossip was permitted only between members of the same sex.

For poor Catharine, etiquette required that a gentleman's attentions to a lady never be too steady or too intimate without purpose, and a lady accept those attentions only if she intended to accept his proposal. To encourage a man for sport, to flirt, was not simply unladylike, it was immoral. How, then, had Catharine found herself in the position of being engaged without wanting to marry the man? As she wrote her sister, she gave her promise "contrary to my judgment."[10] Why?

For women, marriage was a social imperative. It was not until 1848 in New York and 1854 in Massachusetts that women were allowed to own property; therefore, a spinster was homeless, penniless, and a social inconvenience. The social and economic benefits of marriage for a woman were so great that it was hard to understand if she turned down an eligible man. Catharine's relatives would not understand, nor would the community, and Catharine could barely understand herself. She wrote, "I am degraded in my own opinion." The only acceptable ground for refusal was the ineligibility of the man.

Etiquette books did not mince words: if her husband were shiftless, profligate, intemperate, or disloyal, she and her children would suffer cold, loneliness, and hunger. If a man chose unwisely, if his wife were not steady, thrifty, virtuous, and able, domestic felicity was impossible.

Catharine's problem was that she was refusing the proposal of a gentleman. A gentleman had knowledge of the world, taste, sense, and goodness.

He was attentive without being intrusive; he was self-aware without being self-centered. He did not act dishonorably or allow his actions or words to be misconstrued as dishonorable. He was not a vulgarian, slangwhanger (demagogue), slugabed (idler) or drunkard. If at all possible, he was wealthy, but at least he was well employed or had prospects.

Catharine was turning down an eligible man, a gentleman even in her own opinion. She wrote her sister, "He deserves ... all the tenderness of your friendship. I beg you to persuade him that the object of his pursuit was not worth the regret of such a noble mind as his."[11]

Catharine had to convince her brother that she was acting in a proper ladylike manner, that she had grounds for her refusal because once her parents were gone, as a spinster, she could not establish her own household but had to seek to be welcomed into his home. On what grounds could she convince her brother that her decision was sound? A lady had good understanding and cool judgment. While some etiquette books required that she never show emotion in public, others simply required that she regulate her emotions. In contradiction, she was required to have strong feelings and an affectionate disposition. It was desirable to be pretty but mandatory to be well turned out. Appropriate dress for every occasion was part of good behavior. She was to be taught and have knowledge, talents, and skills but never be clever or opinionated.

So first, Catharine was contrite and self-effacing. Then she found refuge in assuring her family she acted in the *gentleman*'s best interests. "I was convinced that Mr. B was made more unhappy by our last summer's engagement for it kept him in a state of emotional agitation."[12] Finally she was not too assertive, but assured her brother that she broke the engagement with her fiancé's consent: "He has been so generous as to relinquish the promise I then gave him and all is now ended forever."[13]

Catharine remained a spinster and became an internationally acclaimed author. Her female characters fought against the advances of men they could not love and frequently broke the boundaries of ladylike behavior. Catharine lived out her days in her brother's household in Lenox.

Other writers have identified Mr. B. as William Cullen Bryant. On March 17, 1817, two years earlier, Bryant wrote a friend, George Downes, "I have heard that you are married. Alas! Sir ... Marriage is a lottery—and little does one know when he chuses the number of his ticket whether it draw a blank or a prize.... I will not disturb your felicity on this occasion with many unlucky reflections of my own upon the subject of marriage."[14]

That may sound like a man who would never marry, but the second letter he wrote that day was to the woman he would marry. It was a chatty, happy, and if it were not ungentlemanly to say so, a flirty letter. It was to a young woman named Frances Fairchild, whom he would court for the next four years and whom he would marry in 1821.

It is implausible to assume that a gentleman courted two women at one time. A better guess for Mr. B. is Stockbridge resident, neighbor, and Sedgwick family friend Cyrus Byington. He was born in a house built by Catharine's father. From humble beginnings, he was taken in and educated by the wealthy and influential Joseph Woodbridge. He became a lawyer and then a minister. In 1819, he professed his heart was set on missionary work. His friend Orville Dewey feared it was a broken heart. Byington left Stockbridge to become a missionary to the Choctaw Indians. He never returned.

American Morals

Many Europeans who visited America were surprised by the contrast with the sexual morality in their homelands. They attributed American morality to religious beliefs, and to the absence of a leisure class: American men were evidently too busy working to have dalliances. They cited the habit in America of marrying early, and to the very construction of the American house, which they believed made it impossible to have an illicit liaison anywhere in the home without everyone knowing it. The eighteenth-century notion of sex in the midst of life was exploded. The nineteenth-century couple demanded privacy, and the morality of American men and women might also have been attributed to discretion.

All was not delicate and decorous. In 1831, it was reported that there were 2,000 prostitutes in Boston. In a total population of approximately 50,000, it was a figure too high for many to believe. However, the police estimated there were 227 "bawdy houses" in Boston, so that was fewer than ten working girls per establishment. The location of the houses of ill repute and the stores that sold pornography and cheap liquor were concentrated in red-light districts isolated from and ignored by polite society. Ladies took a position that reflected the geography: they knew Five Points and the Tenderloin existed in New York City; they knew of Ann Street (the Black Sea) in Boston, but they never went there or acknowledged their existences.

That became harder to do when the sensational murders of prostitutes during the 1830s and 1840s focused a spotlight on this population and affected both the law and journalism. Both were forced to take note and act—one by reporting the sordid details and calling for reform, the other by passing laws in an attempt to legislate reform.

Men frequented prostitutes. It was acceptable for a man, single or married, to have affairs. The burden for morality at home had shifted to the wife. Yet it was not true that the obligation to uphold morals was the sole province of the women. Men who indulged were required to exercise extreme care. The evil of prostitution was never to "cross the domestic threshold or trouble family life." If a man allowed his private affairs to become public, he was excluded from society—all doors shut to him. Affairs remained acceptable only when they were segregated from his life as husband or suitor. Such affairs were never spoken of in polite society, and the recipient of a gentleman's sexual advances was never a respectable woman, a social peer, a member of the gentleman's social circle, or a married woman. The line not to be crossed was bright and well understood. Proof was not required; behavior or loose talk that bred suspicion was sufficient.

Based on a fallacy, the freedoms allowed men and women were very different. It was considered natural for men to experience sexual passion and acceptable for them to act on it. Decent women, it was believed, experienced only platonic and maternal love. Furthermore, if a gentleman overstepped into violence or public disgrace, it was assumed that the woman had tempted him into evil as Eve did Adam. Therefore it was never acceptable for a woman, single or married, to have an affair, but a philandering man could remain in good standing socially if he observed the rules. The domestic hearth was sacrosanct. If a man acted at the expense of conjugal fidelity—that is, if he seduced another man's wife—he was banished from society, and so was the lady. The instances of interfering with someone else's wife were rare. When it occurred, the family, friends, and the entire social circle moved to intervene.

The currents that move the masses were shifting. Change was coming. By mid-century the population grew from 5 million to over 20 million, and more Americans were moving to cities. Love was idealized, and rejection of predestination sparked a desire to create a happy life on earth. Waiting for the afterlife, delayed gratification, was the stuff of the last century. The etiquette book was replacing religious tracks. The novel was replacing advice from the older women.

In 1876 Judge Julius Rockwell, a man who dedicated a lifetime to adherence to the law and promotion of social decency, wrote his wife in a huff:

> *My dearest Lucy . . . It has been ascertained that about 6/7th of books taken from libraries everywhere are sensation novels. . . . A girl may read [these books] a thousand years and never know as much as her grandmother did after she read just a few decent books.*[15]

But the young girls were not listening, perhaps not even his wife. Things were changing for women—not as a function of the law, politics, or even philosophy, but as a function of economics. There was a machine in the new Garden of Eden creating wealth that could buy a piece of heaven on earth. Jefferson's agricultural utopia would become industrialized. Women would travel far beyond hearth and home. The city would offer them more than jobs. There would be shops where store-bought was preferred to homespun, markets that would offer more than any kitchen garden, and department stores with more goods in one building than in an entire New England village. The production officer of the old homestead would become the chief consumer. There would be theaters broaching subjects not whispered in the parlor. It was a new century, and while women's advances and retreats approximated a dance more than a forward march, in the new century, there would be no baby girls named Submit.

Appendix I:

Importance of the French and Indian War

. . . To distress by every means Available . . .
—GOVERNOR WILLIAM SHIRLEY, 1755

War was officially declared in May 1756, but battles in the French and Indian War began years before. The fear engendered by the early skirmishes can hardly be exaggerated.

To protect Pittsfield from early raids, Col. William Williams built Fort Anson in 1754. It was built by the simple expedient of fortifying his home. The house was 40 x 24 feet, the storehouse 10 x 35; there was a chamber for a soldier's lodging, a well, and a yard that was clad—that is, the dirt was covered with wood planks. The whole area was surrounded by a 14-foot-high fence. Topping the fence at two points were watch towers. The cost of building, initially laid out by Williams, was reported to be 91 pounds. The inhabitants protected by Fort Anson agreed to work the land in common and share with the soldiers who manned it.

The advent of war did nothing to ameliorate earlier fears. Col. Israel Williams was the commander of the Hampshire militia. He was both William Williams's commanding officer and his uncle. In 1756, Israel wrote William: "My poor neighbors are trembling with fear for what is a coming."[1]

Both the French and the British recruited Indians to fight on their side. It presented an interesting problem. In 1756, a British general warned his troops: "It is very necessary to keep a good lookout at all times. The only risk will be our people may make a mistake and fire upon our own Indians. Should such a misfortune happen, it would cause great uneasiness."[2]

The French and Indian War was the North American battlefield of a larger war between Britain and France called the Seven Year War. Perhaps for that reason, or some other, the British were parsimonious regarding payment to their Indian allies, and money for frontier fortifications. Of the 91 pounds to build Fort Anson, William was reimbursed 63 pounds.

On September 17, 1755, Williams complained to the command center in Albany that he had hired men, including Indians, to fulfill their orders to build Fort Williams and to move provisions from the "carrying place" to the fort. Indians traveled by water, and the carrying place was literally the place at which they carried their boats across land from one waterway to another. Williams wrote: "I borrowed some hundreds to pay them [the Indians] and considerable is still due to them. I sent down an account to Albany, and either through forgetfulness or the multiplicity of business, it has lain unnoticed."[3]

In 1755, the governor of the Massachusetts province, William Shirley, allotted funds to create a light infantry, trained them to fight in the Massachusetts terrain, and charged them "To distress by every means available the French in their settlements and their allies."[4]

The British army was contemptuous of the colonial militia. They were wrong. Historians credit the militia with tilting the war in favor of the British.

The colonials were equally contemptuous of the British. Israel Williams wrote:

> *This country is in [jeopardy] of falling into the hands of the French ... the English do as their grandfathers did, they make good votes respecting their affairs but they do not put them in execution. ... I am quite sick of past schemes and their execution and since I can't help to any purpose I content myself with lamenting our dark and dreadful state and condition.*[5]

Israel encouraged Williams to build a second fort in Pittsfield. Fort Ashley would protect an additional section of the village, and would offer "the advantages that would arise from a fortress on the height of land." Israel did not believe the British would understand the advantage of a string of fortifications any more than they understood the advantage of a light infantry.

> *I despair of obtaining succor from our government for our frontiers—they are very much winked out of sight. If you think it best and prudent to stir that matter, I shall be glad. I am sure it is of some importance that the avenues to us be stopped and New York not be the sole object of care.*[6]

Much less is written about the French and Indian War than the Revolutionary War when, in fact, there were strong connections. The British won the Seven Year War with France at a terrible price. Swimming in debt, they heavily taxed the colonies. In part, the increased taxation led to the Revolutionary War. Once war was declared, the way it was fought and by whom was influenced by the French and Indian War. It is true that when a formal decision was made, the new country decided in favor of a Continental army rather than a militia, but the light infantry developed in the French and Indian War in Massachusetts, called the citizen militia and the people's army, had some influence on how the Revolutionary War was fought and won.

Appendix II:

The Revolutionary War and Property Confiscation

We passed a pleasant social day at Colonel Larned's friendly mansion.[1]

When someone loses their property today, we think foreclosure, but in the early days in Pittsfield, there were others ways to lose property. One lot, 359 East Street (the William Russell Allen House today) is a good example of the different grounds for seizure and of the shifting fortunes of men. Over one hundred years (1749–1849), there were three owners who bought and then lost the land, and one who got it back—sort of.

The first owner was Elisha Jones, a Tory. Not much is known about Jones because he was an absentee owner. We can assume, however, that he was well placed politically, and well heeled, because he was awarded a chunk of Western Massachusetts by the General Court in 1749. Those very political connections would cost him his land.

Just prior to and during the Revolutionary War, Tory land was confiscated and the "disaffected" asked to leave, in exchange for their liberty. Jones was an absentee owner, so in 1775, it was easy for his neighbor, Charles Goodrich, to seize Jones's land and thereby extend his property line.

Goodrich was an original settler of Pittsfield. He was appointed one of the commissioners who partitioned Poontoosuck. It was Charles Goodrich who requested Joseph Dwight Esquire to call the first town meeting. Goodrich brought Reverend Thomas Allen to Pittsfield, and sat on the committee "to manage the whole affair of the meeting house."

Ironically, a year after Goodrich seized Jones's land, in June 1776 Goodrich was accused of being "inimical to his country" because "he procured himself a commission in the king's name . . . as a justice of the peace [thereby] submitting to British authority." Goodrich was assessed both public and private damages. His property might have been seized to pay the damages and because he "joined with Tories." However, Goodrich fought back. He claimed his character was "maliciously stabbed," there was no truth to the accusations, and he deserved damages. In January 1779, the matter was arbitrated at the Eastman Tavern. A compromise was struck. Goodrich did better than Jones, and better than the next owner: he was assessed the cost of the arbitration but retained his property. In 1788, Charles Goodrich sold the land to Colonel Simon Larned (or Learned)—just in time for Mary Gray Bidwell to visit.

Appendix III:

The Revolutionary War and the Constitutionalists

... a statement of the unhappy circumstances
in this distracted county ...[1]

During the Revolutionary War, Pittsfield, and all but two Berkshire villages, was divorced from Boston. Berkshire County did not allow the state courts to sit from 1775 to 1781 nor would it send representatives to Boston.

The rebellious Constitutionalists demanded a state constitution before they would acknowledge state laws. The anti-Constitutionalists, who wanted to operate under provincial law in the interim, warned Boston that there would be anarchy and "the unhappy circumstances in this distracted county."

Though they wrote *distracted*, the anti-Constitutionalists meant *demented*. The question is: Were they right? Did Pittsfield sink into lawlessness?

The short answer is: no. The local government was so strong, it hardly missed a beat. At the town meeting, the selectmen, the treasurer, the clerk, the moderator, and the people filled the gap left by the state courts and state officials. They added to the number of constables: In Pittsfield they were Eli Root, David Bush, Major Stoddard (later replaced by John Remington), John Strong, and Joseph Wright. They established committees: the Committee of Inspection "empowered to regulate quarrels and disturbances"; the Committee of Safety to punish crime; the Committee of Accounts "to keep a true account of all warlike stores supplied"; and the Committee of Correspondence, initially to communicate any imminent danger to the local community, later became the vehicle to state and restate to Boston the Berkshire position and demand for a constitution.

The Committees of Inspection and Safety assumed the roles of civil and criminal courts, respectively. They heard cases in local taverns. The cases brought were most often boundary disputes, land transfer and sale disputes, outstanding bills, and a number of suits for slander. These last were so numerous, probably, because it was a time of war, and the penalty for disloyalty could be heavy. If someone was called a Tory and it was found to be true, the result was imprisonment and seizure of property.

Anti-Constitutionalists and Constitutionalists were constantly hurling insults, and some rose to the level of slander. To mediate, mitigate, or punish, there were the committees and also the Board of Arbitration and the Congregational Church.

With their predictions of dire consequences proven untrue, the anti-Constitutionalists retaliated in informal ways. Lavinia Deane and the Reverend Monson were caught in the crossfire.

Appendix IV:

Eighteenth-Century Political Parties

It was 1800; Pittsfield was thirty-nine years old. With a population of 2,261, Pittsfield had grown more than 10 percent in ten years and was the largest town in Berkshire County. The Reverend Allen had been in the pulpit for thirty-seven years, and ten years hence, Allen would be dead. It was then that opposition to Allen began in earnest and grew. It culminated in Woodbridge Little, lawyer and Federalist, writing the document that attempted to unseat Allen and succeeded in splitting the Pittsfield Congregational Church in two.

The Federalists were the first political party in America. For the better part of twenty-five years, the critical first twenty-five years of the Republic, the Federalists held sway over national policy. They were for a strong federal government, a conciliatory attitude toward the British, and strong fiscal policy including strong central banks.

Their opponents were alternately called the Democrats, Republicans, Jeffersonians, or just plain anti-Federalists. They interpreted the Federalist position as the preamble to returning to, if not a monarchy, at least an elitist society. The political divide was sharp and political battles were hot. To avoid bloodshed, the Federalists and anti-Federalists built different taverns in which to drink, and preferred to read different newspapers.

The battle between Federalists and anti-Federalists was longstanding in 1800, so why did Pittsfield rise up at that time against its decidedly Jeffersonian pastor? It was clear twenty-five years earlier that Allen was, if not a rebel, then an independent thinker. It was Allen who led the county and the Constitutionalists in the successful revolt against Boston that forced a state constitution. Everyone knew then (1775–1781) that

Allen was guided by Jeffersonian principles of democracy and by another anti-Federalist, Patrick Henry. During those six years he was revered as a leader and brave man.

Eleven years later, in 1792, there was a brief reprimand issued when Allen wrote articles for an anti-Federalist newspaper. Congregants complained that he should not take time away from his duties to write the articles and that he introduced "affairs of state" into his sermons. The formal accusation: "The Reverend Mr. Allen having in times past, in his official character, repeatedly interested himself in the political affairs of the country, and publically interposed therein in an undue and improper manner." The complaint was quickly resolved because of the popular acceptance of Allen as their pastor. The resolution of the matter stated: "We consider Mr. Allen to be liable to human frailties and error ... but we by no means charge him with any sinister or criminal intention therein."[1]

In 1792, the grumbling was handled with dispatch and died away. Not so in the 1800s. In 1800, the Federalists lost decisively in national elections; that year, the most outspoken and eloquent anti-Federalist, Thomas Jefferson, became president of the United States. Perhaps the Federalists didn't know it then but they would never rise to power again. In the first blush of defeat, the Federalists clung together, redoubled their efforts to win converts to their political beliefs, and were very vocal in their opposition to Jefferson. Pittsfield Federalists demanded that their pastor stop using the pulpit to support Jefferson and his allies. In Pittsfield, the longtime battle between Federalists and anti-Federalists graduated from hot to sizzling with Allen as the focal point.

Early on, Allen had linked democracy and Christianity in his mind. The Federalists' monarchical leanings were anathema to him. Further, Allen would not accept any limits to his right to speak his mind from the pulpit—in this he was not alone. New England ministers had long claimed the right to speak from the pulpit on any issue of the day, political or otherwise.

So Allen preached and the Federalists fumed from 1800 to 1806. That year, Woodbridge Little took up his pen and wrote: "Your discourses generally ... were interlarded with politics ... most pointedly irritating and insulting and caused very general uneasiness in the town."[2] Little demanded satisfaction, and Allen replied: "[you] have left me completely in the dark as to what you would be pleased to deem adequate and reasonable satisfaction. . . . You will, therefore, be pleased to tell me what satisfaction will be agreeable to you." Allen's response satisfied no one.

The dissatisfied requested a meeting of the whole church to resolve the issue. Allen declined. Little then wrote the Association of Congregational ministers, who rebuffed him in the following words: "We are of the opinion that for any members of the church to unite together in measures that implicate the character of your pastor, either as unchristian or imprudent, is an unjustifiable step."[3]

Then the unexpected happened, and the Federalists quickly took advantage. The governor of Massachusetts visited Pittsfield and during the night some people burned his image in effigy. The local Federalist newspaper named Allen as one of the instigators. It was 1808, and Allen was sixty-six and in poor health. He attempted to reconcile with Little and attempted to clear his name of the false charge, but it was too late. Many had already left the church. That winter, Little and 108 others made application to Boston to form a new parish. It passed the House of Representatives unchallenged, and the Union Congregational Parish of Pittsfield was formed.

In Stockbridge the Federalists had stewed long enough about their defector, Barnabas Bidwell. In power locally, they acted and issued a warrant for his arrest for irregularities in the Treasurer's office. Locally the Federalists were cleaning house, but they would never rise to power again nationally.

Appendix V:

The Constitutionalists and Shays' Regulators: A Comparison

Some historians compare the Berkshire Constitutionalists and Daniel Shays' Rebellion as two stops on the road to the federal constitution of 1787. Actually they are far easier to contrast. The Constitutionalists were Berkshire's own; Shays' Rebellion started in Hampshire County. The Constitutionalists closed the courts as a symbol of their rejection of state authority unless and until there was a state constitution. The Constitutionalists believed that until there was a state constitution, they had no legal basis to rule. Shays closed the courts and freed prisoners to stop "debt" trials wherein farms were repossessed and debtors imprisoned. They were rebelling against state rule after there was a state constitution and legitimate basis to rule. The Constitutionalists used powerful words and maintained the peace; Shays' men used weapons and broke the law. The Constitutionalists were rebelling as the Revolutionary War began; Shays was rebelling after the war had been won.

Appendix VI:

Weakening of the Church

Nothing is as cheap as milk and ministers.[1]

If there was a group the power elite in the community kept a sharp eye on, it was their ministers. When William Williams wrote that "Ashley came to Sheffield with less money than your minister," he was using a familiar example to make his point: Everyone in the eighteenth century knew ministers were poor. They were also cheap to purchase. While it was important what they preached, it was easy to replace them if their message chafed. More and more the civil authority was pressuring the ecclesiastic authority to reflect their values, and their politics.

In the end, the single outstanding characteristic of his ministry was that the Reverend Mr. Monson lasted in Lenox, Massachusetts, for twenty-two years. Samuel Monson graduated from Yale in 1763. In October 1770 Monson was given "a call to settle in the work of the Gospel ministry."[2] On November 11, 1770, Monson was ordained the first Congregational minister in Lenox.

In the eighteenth century, in order to be incorporated as a town, places in Massachusetts were required to hire a Congregational minister. The business of the towns and the business of the churches were inexorably bound, so the salary of the minister was decided in town meeting, the town selectmen were often the deacons of the church, ministers preached political views from the pulpit, and sins in the church were crimes in the court.

Monson's ministry in Lenox began well. The town voted "50 shillings and 24 pence for entertaining the minister and delegates at the ordination."

Monson was given a salary of 45 pounds with a promise of annual increases, and a grant of land, the minister's lot. Then things changed.

By 1778, it became a contentious relationship. Records of the town meetings are replete with reports of conflicts between Monson and his flock. There was a debate, almost annually, about his compensation. He was paid partly in firewood, and the amount of wood was reduced in proportion to the congregants' displeasure. That may seem a small act, even insignificant, unless you have spent a winter in the Berkshires without adequate heat.

It was easier to drive a minister out than fire him, or in this case freeze him out. However, Monson would not go.

Oddly, nowhere is the origin of the conflict spelled out. For fourteen of his twenty-two years in Lenox there were hushed grumblings and loud outbursts between minister and town of undetermined origin.

In August 1792, the congregation evidently reached the limit of its patience, and it brought a complaint to the Ecclesiastical Council. The council was akin to a trial court and the complaint akin to a charge. If Monson were censured, found guilty, then the town could remove him. So would the origin of the dissatisfaction finally be clearly stated?

The charges were: "a degree of passion unworthy in the ministerial character; speaking with such levity and inconsideration as approaches slander, and showing a disposition for the worldly." To modern ears, it sounds like sex, lies, and rock and roll. In fact these were charges that struck at the heart of the covenant.

The first charge, "a degree of passion," accused the minister of acting and speaking with passion as opposed to subjecting his behavior to reason, regulation, and God's will. The second charge related to a tenet of the church that "God should condemn all levity" because levity spoke of inconstancy and unsteadiness in commitment to the church. The final charge, "a disposition for the worldly," referred to forbidden entertainments such as dancing and singing, and the pursuit of worldly gain. Pursuit of gain was condemned because the true pursuits were spiritual— "those who set their hearts on the things of the world" were not sincere in their commitment to God. So the charge was the most serious that could be levied: The Reverend Monson was not a good Christian.

Was the minister not a good Christian and was that the origin of the fourteen years of dissatisfaction? Probably not. Other contemporary writers described Monson as "a man of good abilities, of ardent piety, sound in the faith, and zealous in promoting the cause of the Redeemer." Moreover the council found that Monson's character was in general that of "a faithful Minister of the Gospel, a man of moral and pious behavior and conduct, who, in the view of the Council, is undeserving of impeachment." Further the council concluded nothing of "a censurable nature is supported by evidence." Nonetheless, within a few months, Lenox fired Monson. So what was the origin of the battle between minister and town?

Monson lived in difficult times. There was the Revolutionary War, the Constitutionalists versus the anti-Constitutionalists, Shays' Rebellion, and the Federalists versus the anti-Federalists, and each divided the people. During the war, there were still those who considered themselves the king's men. Those fighting for a Massachusetts constitution approved by the people were ardently opposed by those who felt the king's provincial laws should remain in place because law and order trumped human rights. Some saw Shays as a criminal while others sympathized with his fight. Finally the Federalists were seen by anti-Federalists as supporters of, if not the restoration of the monarchy, then institution of a firm socioeconomic hierarchy. If Monson and the congregants were on opposite sides of these issues then Monson's interest in worldly pursuits was an interest in politics, his passion not subdued by reason was his expression of opinions that differed from his detractors, and his levity which approached slander, may have been his accusation of those on the other side.

Politics and religion were inexorably bound in Massachusetts. Unity and order were becoming more aspiration than reality. Fights between minister and town were like the signal fires of the war to come.

From the outset, there was a potential for conflict: The people might see the minister as a town employee; the minister might see himself, as Reverend West did, as possessor of God's word superior to any law. What they wanted, at other times, was their minister to, frankly, lighten up.

His name was Samuel Hopkins. On September 9, 1743, the proprietors of the land between Upper Housatonic (Sheffield) and the Indian land (Stockbridge) voted "to give Mr. Samuel Hopkins a call to settle with us in the work of the Gospel Ministry; to give Mr. Hopkins 35 pounds lawful money per annum for the first five years, 45 pounds thereafter to enable him to go on with his work, and 60 pounds lawful money for his settlement."

Hopkins accepted the position on November 25, 1743: "I do now find myself disposed and willing to comply with your desires." So on December 28, 1743, Samuel Hopkins was ordained pastor of the First Congregational Church of Great Barrington (at that time called the Second Congregational Church of Sheffield).

At his ordination, there were as many pastors officiating from the Congregational churches in Springfield, Westfield, Sheffield, Stockbridge, and Northampton as there were congregants—five. Hopkins served as pastor for twenty-five years, and during that time the congregation grew from 5 to 17 members in the first year and to 116 members by 1768.

It was, in many ways, an uneasy alliance. Hopkins was sad to leave his teacher and mentor, Jonathan Edwards, in Northampton and settle at such a distance. His religious sentiments were strongly Calvinistic, essentially the same as Edwards's. The population was somewhat more relaxed and more diversified. It was reported that there were more taverns in the place than churches, and that attendance at the taverns was more religious. It was a report made with a scowl of disapproval by some and a chortle of glee by others.

Hopkins wrote: "The revival that has come down on many of the New England churches like showers that water the earth appears to have passed by Great Barrington." Hopkins reported experiencing "trials and discouragement, darkness and despondency." The revival or "Great Awakening" was the very doctrine that had hobbled John Fisk in his effort to wed the Widow Deane.

Hopkins's lot in Great Barrington was not one of unremitting sadness. In 1748 Hopkins married Joanna, daughter of Moses Ingersoll, the first tavern owner in Great Barrington. After John Sergeant's death, in 1751, Hopkins was offered the position of pastor and elder of the First Congregational Church of Stockbridge. He turned down the position and was instrumental in bringing Jonathan Edwards to Stockbridge to fill it. For five years, Hopkins's beloved teacher was in the next village. When

Edwards left for Princeton, Hopkins and his replacement, Stephen West, became close friends.

During this time Hopkins was highly esteemed for his "strength of mental powers" by intelligentsia in Boston but not as much in Great Barrington. Every few years he placed himself before the congregation and offered his resignation; they never accepted it, but sadly it may have been for lack of interest. Finally in 1768, Hopkins submitted his resignation and it was accepted. He did so because for the preceding five years, Great Barrington had not paid his salary. There has been a longstanding argument about whether Hopkins was fired or quit—nonpayment for five years may offer the definitive answer.

Hopkins left, and for eighteen years, there was no replacement hired nor was Hopkins's departure mourned. It was a century later, at the close of another war, that his worth was acclaimed, his accomplishments celebrated. The Reverend Hopkins was proclaimed the first person in New England to take a stand against slavery.

In one of his many sermons, Hopkins asked: "If we obstinately refuse to reform what we know to be wrong . . . the holding of the Africans in slavery . . . have we not great reason to fear that God will withdraw his protection and punish us?"[3]

It took a hundred years and a civil war for Hopkins to receive any praise. Monson slipped away and off the pages of history. Even the great and revered Stephen West was excommunicated, as was his wife for drinking to intoxication. The minister who served in his pulpit for forty-six years relatively unmolested was the most political, most revolutionary, most militaristic, and most materialistic of them all. In the end that would be very good for women.

In December 1763, Goodrich and Crofut, on behalf of the newly incorporated town, invited Thomas Allen of Northampton, a twenty-year-old theology student, to preach as a probationer. Allen's grandfather, Joseph Allen, was a deacon and close friend of Reverend Jonathan Edwards, who was considered the greatest theologian of his day. Allen was one of ten children, six of whom lived to adulthood. The family was not wealthy, but an uncle provided the funds for Allen to attend and graduate from Harvard.

Young Allen preached, and was warmly received. On the 7th of February 1764, eight men gathered in the house of Deacon Crofut, and signed a confession of faith and a covenant. The covenant was to the faith and to complete the work of building a new and larger meetinghouse. The result would be the Church of Christ, Pittsfield. (In 1790, an even larger church was built, designed by Bullfinch.)

To help in the selection of a pastor and the design of the church, the Pittsfield men invited preachers from other Berkshire towns: the Reverend Samuel Hopkins of Great Barrington, whom Harriet Beecher Stowe immortalized in *The Minister's Wooing*; Dr. Stephen West of Stockbridge, a man of great note in his day; and the eminent Reverend Ebenezer Martin of Becket. During the next meeting on March 5, 1764, they determined to call Allen to the pastorate.

Allen responded in the following letter:

To the People of Pittsfield: Dear Brethren,
Your invitation of me to settle among you in the gospel ministry I
have received by your committee chosen for that purpose; I apprehend
I have duly considered the same. In answer to this, your invitation,
I would say, that having sought divine direction, taken the advice
of the judicious, and duly consulted my own judgment, I cannot
but think it my duty to accept; and, accordingly, do now declare my
cordial acceptance of the same. I take this opportunity to testify my
grateful sense of your respect, shown in that good agreement and har-
mony that subsisted among you in the choice of one less than the least
of all saints, to preach among you the unsearchable riches of Christ.[4]

In his letter of acceptance he spoke of the being "the least of all saints" committed to "preach among you." Allen was a sincerely religious man dedicated to finding "the unsearchable riches of Christ," but he was a judicious man interested in the attainable riches of this world. His letter ended:

Nothing doubting but that, at your next meeting, you will freely
grant forty or fifty cords of wood annually, or as much as you shall

think sufficient, and some addition to my settlement, either by grant in work, or whatever, out of generosity, by subscription or whatever way you please, I now stand ready to be introduced to the work whereunto I am called, as soon as a convenient opportunity shall present itself. These from your affectionate friend, Thomas Allen[5]

On April 18, 1764, Allen was installed as the first minister at Pittsfield. Well educated, young, and fiery, Reverend Allen took possession of the minister's lot. He also had an "old gig" (horse and wagon) to drive around the four square miles of his parish.

He was a practical man seeking to adequately support his wife, Elizabeth, and, as their family grew, his twelve children. He did not find any contradiction between God's work and man's. Not surprisingly, this practical man surveyed his town and looked with favor upon its manufacturing and concomitant mercantile growth. J. E. A. Smith describes him as a man with "clear foresight resulting from native acumen and thorough study of the natural advantages of the home which he loved."

Bibliography

Acts and Laws of His Majesty's English Colony (New London CT, 1750–1771).

Carol Berkin, *Independence* (New York: Alfred A. Knopf, 2005.

Carol Berkin, *Revolutionary Mothers: Women in the Struggle for America's Independence* (New York: Vintage Books, 2005).

Carol Berkin, and Mary Beth Norton. *Women of America* (Boston: Houghton Mifflin, 1979).

Melissa Bohrer, *Glory Passion and Principle* (New York: Atria Books, 2003).

Alice Morse Earle, *Home Life in Colonial Days* (New York: Macmillan, 1898).

Elizabeth Fries Ellet, *The Women of the American Revolution* (Volume 1, NY: Baker & Scribner, 1848; Volume 2, Baker & Scribner, 1850).

Thomas A. Foster, *Sex and the Eighteenth Century Man* (Boston: Beacon Press, 2006).

George Washington's Rules of Civility & Decent Behavior, Colonial Williamsburg Foundation. Williamsburg, VA: Beaver Press, 1971.

Phebe A. Hanaford, *Daughters of America, or, Women of the Century* (Augusta, ME and Washington, DC: DAR, 1849; Charleston, NC: Nabu Press, 2011).

Carol F. Karlsen and Laurie Crumpacker, eds., *The Journal of Esther Edwards Burr 1754–1757* (New Haven, CT: Yale University Press, 1984).

Vera Laska, *Remember the Ladies: Outstanding Women of the American Revolution* (Boston: Commonwealth of Massachusetts Bicentennial Commission Publication, 1975).

Pauline Moody, "Deborah Sampson," chapter 7 of *Sharon, Massachusetts—A History,* http://sharonhistoricalsociety.org/All_Else/All_Pages/DEBORAH%20SAMPSON.pdf (1975).

Alice Morse, *Colonial Dames and Good Wives* (Boston: Houghton Mifflin & Co., 1895).

Mary Beth Norton, *Liberty's Daughter* (Ithaca, NY: Cornell University Press, 1980).

Mary Beth Sievens, *Stray Wives* (New York: New York University Press, 2005).

Laurel Thatcher Ulrich, *Good Wives* (New York: Vintage Press, 1991).

Philip Young, *Revolutionary Ladies* (New York: Alfred A. Knopf, 1977).

Endnotes

Chapter 1 Introduction

1   Mary Beth Norton, *Liberty's Daughters*. Ithaca, NY: Cornell University Press, 1996, p. 4, from a letter written by Ann Page to Elizabeth Randolph, November 6, 1801.

2   The estimate of literate men varies from 40 to 65 percent in one report and as high as 75 percent in another. More white men in New England than in the southern colonies could read and write; no statistic includes nonwhites. The definition of the term *literate* is important. It meant only that the man could sign his name legibly and could read; it did not mean he was well read.

3   In *Thomas Gardner, Planter, and Some of His Descendants*, privately printed 1933, F. A. Gardner wrote, "Thomas Gardner was indeed slighted by history . . . he not John Winthrop was the first governor of Massachusetts."

4   Francis Bremer, *John Winthrop: America's Forgotten Founding Father*. New York: Oxford University Press, 2003, p. 321.

5   An ordinary title of respect granted a married woman, Goodwife was often shortened to Goody.

6   Cotton Mather, *Ornaments for the Daughter of Zion*. Ann Arbor: Text Creation Partnership, 2005–12; Reprint, Delmar NY: Scholars Facsimiles & Reprints, 1978.

Chapter 2 The Homestead

1   Lewis Carroll, *Through the Looking Glass*, "The Knight's Tale." London: Macmillan, 1871.

2   *Journal of Lieutenant Isaac Bangs April 1–July 29, 1776*, ed. Edward Bangs. Cambridge: John Wilson & Son, 1890, p. 51.

3 Ibid.

4 Ibid., p. 62.

5 Ibid.

6 Ibid.

7 Ibid.

8 Richard Bidwell Wilcox, private collection.

9 William Fowler, "The Historical Status of the Negro in Connecticut," *Historical Magazine*, January 1884: 13.

10 Kenneth Minkemma, "Jonathan Edwards on Slavery and the Slave Trade," *The William & Mary Quarterly*, 3rd Series, 54:4, October 1997, p. 825.

11 Ibid., p. 832. However, as Minkemma points out, Edwards's position was nuanced. He opposed the slave trade and the selling of free men into slavery while owning slaves and recognizing slavery.

12 *The Dublin Seminar for New England Folk-life*, Annual Proceedings 1988, Boston University, "Provisions for Daughters: The Accounts of Samuel Lane," 1988, p. 11.

13 Ibid.

14 Ibid., p. 12.

15 Ibid.

16 Bed curtains surrounded the bed. They were hung just as window curtains were, on rods on all four sides of the bed. Pulled closed at night, they provided both privacy and additional warmth.

17 Land that then cost $8,900 could cost from $142,500 to $569,000 today. Estimates of equivalent values vary. Some experts multiply by as much as 64 or as little as 16 to approximate current value. These equivalent amounts are inserted so the reader is not misled by what appear to be very small amounts and should be taken as approximations only.

18 Carol F. Karlsen and Laurie .Crumpacker, eds. *The Journal of Esther Edwards Burr*, New Haven, CT: Yale University Press, 1984, p. 24.

19 Approximately $3,200–$12,800 today.

20 *Journal of Esther Edwards Burr*, Letter # 9, October 5, 1754, p. 49.

21 Ibid.

22 Ibid., October 6, 1754, p. 51.

23 Alice Morse Earle, *Home Life in Colonial Days*. New York: Macmillan, 1926; reprint, Readaclassic.com, 2009, p. 155.

24 *Intimate conversation* was a term for marital sexual intercourse; *criminal conversation* was a term for adultery.

25 *Spectator Magazine*, a London daily, March 1711–December 1712, eds. Richard Steele and Joseph Addison.

26 Thomas A. Foster, *Sex and the Eighteenth Century Man*. Boston: Beacon Press, 2006, p. 23.

27 William Williams Collection of Pittsfield and Berkshire Historical Papers, compiled by Thomas Colt 1823–1876, Berkshire Athenaeum, transcript, p. 69.

28 Rollin H. Cooke Collection, "Pittsfield Mass Church and Other Records," Berkshire Athenaeum, volume 26.

29 Electa F. Jones, *Stockbridge Past and Present*. Springfield, MA: Samuel Bowles & Co., 1854.

30 *Journal of Esther Edwards Burr*, September 2–3, 1756, p. 220.

31 Ibid., September 8, 1756, p. 221.

32 Ibid., September 13, 1756, p. 223.

33 *Correspondence of William Shirley*, ed. Charles Henry Lincoln, 1912, p. 86, Israel Williams to William Shirley, September 12, 1754.

Chapter 3 The Church

1 Rollin H. Cooke Collection, Berkshire Athenaeum, "Meetings and Proceedings of the Church during the Ministry of Dr. West." January 20, 1777, p. 78.

2 The church was not a building. In the eighteenth century the word *church* meant the body of members, what we would call the congregation. The building was called the meetinghouse.

3 Van Schaack fought for religious freedom and tolerance until he emerged victorious in 1792. Van Schaack had been a member of the Dutch Reform Church in New York and an Episcopalian in Massachusetts. In Pittsfield, Massachusetts, all residents were taxed for the support of the Congregational Church and minister's salary. In addition he was assigned and charged for a pew. Van Schaack

objected on the grounds that it was in conflict with the freedom of worship granted by the Constitution. Laughed out of state and local courts, he eventually won his point in the Supreme Court.

4 "Records of the Church of Christ Stockbridge Mass from June 1759 to August 1819," Berkshire Athenaeum, Confession of Faith, p. 4.

5 Ibid., p. 5.

6 "Ministry of Dr. West," November 9, 1769, p. 73.

7 "The Confession, Covenants and Standing Rules of the Church in Stockbridge." Stockbridge, MA: Charles Webster, 1827, Berkshire Athenaeum, V 974.43 St10.

8 Ibid.

9 Ibid.

10 "Confession, Covenants and Standing Rules."

11 Rollin H. Cooke Collection, Berkshire Athenaeum, Sheffield Congregational Church, June 1799, p. 37.

12 Stephen West, "A Vindication of the Principles and Conduct of the Church in Stockbridge." Hartford, CT: Hudson & Goodwin, 1780, p. 88. Berkshire Athenaeum, IN V 974.43 St10.

13 Rollin H. Cooke Collection, Berkshire Athenaeum, Records of the Congregational Church, Great Barrington, November 23, 1769.

14 Approximately $938/month in today's dollars.

15 Lavinia's last name was spelled Higgbee, Higbee, Higby, and Higbey, just as her married name was spelled Dean and Deane. Alternate spellings, especially of names, were not unusual in the eighteenth century. In each case here, one spelling is selected for clarity—in this text, Higby and Deane.

16 A copy of the "Inventory of the estate of Daniel Higgbee late of Sheffield" is available at the Sheffield Historical Society; 167 pounds is equal to approximately $200,000 today.

17 Berkshire County Probate Court, Will, Docket # 741 & # 749.

18 Record of the Church of Christ, vol. 1, "Baptismal Records."

19 Approximately $2 million in today's dollars (ten times the Higby estate).

20 All documentation of the entire Deane Fisk case from admonition to excommunication to the Ecclesiastical Council at Stockbridge

can be found at Berkshire Athenaeum, V. 974.43 St10, "Stockbridge Miscellany," and in the following tracts and pamphlets: John Bacon, *Letter, To the Reverend Joseph Huntington*, D.D. Boston: Nathaniel Willis, 1777; A Gentleman of Connecticut [The Reverend Joseph Huntington], *A Plea Before The Ecclesiastical Council at Stockbridge.* Boston: N. Coverly and R. Hodge [in Newbury-Street, near the Sign of the Lamb], 1782; Stephen West, Pastor, *A Vindication of the Principles and Conduct of the Church in Stockbridge*; John Bacon, *Appendix*, Hartford: Hudson and Goodwin, 1780, *Illustrations of the preceding Letters Drawn from Recent Examples*; The Reverend David D. Field, *An Historical Sketch of the Congregational Church in Stockbridge, MA*. New York: John A. Gray, 1853. All the quotes in the section "Excommunication: The Widow Deane" are taken from these and from the Rollin H. Cooke Collection, "Church of Christ at Stockbridge."

21 Stockbridge Bowl, Lake Mahkeenac, was referred to as the Great Pond in eighteenth-century Stockbridge.

22 Lavinia would have six children with Fisk. As with Deane, she had a child every two years: John Deane Fisk 11/4/1777; Cathy 8/2/1779; Claudius Victory 4/28/1781; Cynthia 5/10/1783; Clarissa 1785; and Claudius Lucius 1787.

23 West, "Vindication of the Principles and Conduct of the Church in Stockbridge."

24 Ibid.

25 Ibid.

26 Theodore M. Hammett, *The Revolutionary Ideology in its Social Context: Berkshire County 1725–1786*. Brandeis University dissertation, 1976, p. 245.

27 J. A. E. Smith, *History of Pittsfield Vol. 1: 1734–1800*. Boston: Lee & Shepard, 1869, p. 327.

28 Ibid.

29 Ibid.

30 Ibid.

31 Ibid., p. 100.

32 Hammett, *The Revolutionary Ideology*, p. 241.

Chapter 4 The Village

1 William Williams Collection, Berkshire Athenaeum vault, Box 2, Document # 227.

2 Ibid.

3 Ibid.

4 Ibid.

5 Pittsfield, Massachusetts, today—the largest town in Berkshire County.

6 "Rights" were ownership or rights to occupy, sell, or lease lands granted by King George through the General Court.

7 She sold the holdings to her nephew William Williams and with them the responsibility to populate Pittsfield. It, in some part, explains the urging to relocate in his letter to his brother-in-law.

8 Inscription on the marble obelisk erected in Sarah Deming's honor in a burial ground on Honasada Street (Williams Street today), Pittsfield.

9 Massachusetts Archives, v. 116, p. 491, letter from Madam Prudence to gentlemen who were residents of Stockbridge in Berkshire County; among them was Ephraim Williams, a relative of William Williams.

10 Lion Miles, *New England Quarterly,* March 1994, "The Red Man Dispossessed," p. 48.

11 *Interval* was a term used in New England meaning "low lying" and called "the plain" in Stockbridge.

12 Survey of the town, 1750, *Indian Proprietorship Book* (IPB) p. 62.

13 Ibid.

14 For more on feme covert see chapter 6.

15 For more on divorce see chapter 6.

16 Miles, *New England Quarterly,* p. 49.

17 Ibid., p. 76.

18 "Court of General sessions held at Great Barrington 4 Sept. 1762: License is granted to Robert Nungkauraut an Indian man of Stockbridge in the County of Berkshire to lease to Elijah Williams Esq., for the term of five hundred years a certain tract of land . . . containing 140 acres."

19 Christina Marquand and Sarah Sedgwick, Stockbridge 1739–1939. Great Barrington, MA: Berkshire Currier, p. 24.

20 The phrase "New England White Village" describes a typical town square with white clapboard buildings.

21 "Confession, Covenants and Standing Rules," pp. 5–6.

22 This is the work of family historian and genealogist Richard Bidwell Wilcox.

23 The population of Boston in the fifty years between 1740 and 1790 ranged from 16,000 to 18,000 with an average of 17,000.

24 West, "Vindication of the Principles and Conduct of the Church in Stockbridge," p. 49.

25 The processes for being accepted into communion and for being excommunicated are discussed in chapter 3.

26 Smith, *Pittsfield*, p. 137. A freehold was the minimum requirement to "abide." A freehold was land granted to a person during his lifetime on which he could pay rent and was usually used as a farm as differentiated from an owner of land or a grantee of a settlement lot within the town.

27 Pittsfield Town Meeting records 1761.

28 Hammett, *The Revolutionary Ideology*, p. 14.

29 Pittsfield Town Meeting records 1780–1782, Berkshire Athenaeum, April 1 & 2, 1782.

30 Larger towns and cities built workhouses: in Pittsfield in 1764, and in Boston in 1662. By 1801 there was need to separate the "vicious poor" from the "worthy poor"; it became customary to build two almshouses in each community.

31 All of Stockbridge in the County of Berkshire who have recently come in to this town for the purpose of abiding therein not having obtained the towns consent therefore that they depart the limits thereof (with their children and others under their care if such they have) within 15 days and of this precept with your doings thereof you are to make return into the office of the Clerk of the town within twenty days next coming that much further proceedings may be had in the premises as the law directs—given under our hand on

this the fifteenth day of June AD 1793. Timothy Edwards Selectman and Ebenezer Cook Constable of Stockbridge.

32 Lenox Town and Selectmen meeting, Minutes 1787, Bound volumes 540–543, Lenox Town Hall.

33 Elmer I. Shepard Collection, Berkshire Athenaeum, Drawer 11,
Stockbridge.

34 The inheritance was 290 pounds in real property and 100 pounds in
personal property—approximately $24,960 today.

35 Court of General Sessions, August 19, 1773, Mass. archives, p. 16.

36 Ibid.

37 Lenox Town and Selectmen meeting.

38 Ibid.

39 Lenox Town and Selectmen meeting.

40 According to the family this poem, "A Rainy Day," was written
in Kingston, Ontario, after Bidwell fled to Canada. Here we take
license with the truth by placing him at his window in Stockbridge,
and perhaps, as he wrote, he was imagining himself there as well.

41 Timothy Edwards, son of Jonathan Edwards, purchased the Main
Street property from the Indians in 1772. Barnabas Bidwell purchased the property from Edwards in 1792. The house and land
would be seized by the Commonwealth of Massachusetts in 1814
after Bidwell fled to Canada ostensibly in repayment of funds ille-
gally taken.

42 Deed executed November 26, 1798, and recorded February 5, 1799
(CBRD, Book 37, page 403).

43 Barnabas Bidwell (poem), circa 1820, Box 1, Folder 42, SML.

44 Alice Morse Earle, *Stage Coach and Tavern Days*. New York: Macmillan Company, 1901, p. 66.

45 See text on criminal conversation, chapters 3 and 6.

46 See chapter 7.

47 Lion Miles, "Anna Bingham from the Red Lion Inn to the Supreme
Court," *New England Quarterly*, June 1996, p. 292, letter to the court
in Springfield in support of Anna Bingham's request for a license
written by town selectmen.

48 Ibid.

49 Records of the Court of Common Pleas 1761–1795, Mass. Archive, p. 716.
50 Petition of Anna Bingham, September 1781, Mass. Archives, 235–353.
51 Lion Miles, "Anna Bingham," p. 293, (Christ admonishing the greedy: you "devour widows' houses").
52 Miles, "Anna Bingham," p. 293.

Chapter 5 The Social Circle

1 Mary Gray to her fiancé Barnabas Bidwell, Yale University, Manuscripts and Archives, February 6, 1792, Box 1 Folder 4.
2 Today this property is part of Tanglewood, the summer home of the Boston Symphony Orchestra.
3 His will provided for a free school—Williams College today.
4 Her father was a colonel who served in the Revolutionary War as Commissary General of the United States for the Northern Department. He was obliged, by declining health, to resign that office and quit the service. He died of consumption, August 25, 1782.
5 Mary to Barnabas, Box 1 Folder 4, February 2, 1792.
6 See part II.
7 The Reverend West's wife Elizabeth was James Gray's first cousin.
8 Mary to Barnabas, January 13, 1807, Box 1, Folder 12.
9 Barnabas to Mary, December 17, 1806, Box 1, Folder 11.
10 Mary to Barnabas, December 23, 1805, Box 1, Folder 8.
11 Mary to Barnabas, December 29, 1806, Box 1, Folder 11
12 National archives, http://founders.archives,gov/documents/Adams/99-03-02-1236, John Adams to John Quincy Adams, February 25, 1804.
13 Mary to Barnabas, January 19, 1805, Box 1, Folder 8. The two political parties were the Federalists and the Republicans; *Democrat* was pejorative for a Republican.
14 Barnabas to Marshall, March 15, 1806, Box 1, Folder 2.
15 Ibid.
16 Mary to Barnabas, January 26, 1806, Box 1, Folder 9.
17 Ibid.

18 Mary to Barnabas, February 26, 1807, Box 1, Folder 12. Marshall was their son, Josiah a nephew they took in.

19 Ibid.

20 Barnabas to Mary, February 13, 1806, Box 1, Folder 9.

21 Vassal White, *Soliloquy on the Death of Mrs. Barnabas Bidwell*, Stockbridge, Massachusetts, 1808, Yale University, Manuscripts and Archives, Box 15, Folder 476.

22 Mary to Barnabas, January 1 1807, Box 1, Folder 12.

23 Barnabas to Mary, January 1, 1807, Box 1, Folder 12.

24 Mary to Barnabas, February 28, 1806, Box 1, Folder 9.

25 A cord of wood is a neat stack four feet high by eight feet wide by four feet deep.

26 Mary to Barnabas, February 26, 1805, Box 1, Folder 8.

27 See chapter 3, "The Church."

28 Vassal White.

29 "A Sketch of the Life and Character of Mrs. Gray," *The Panoplist and Missionary Magazine United, Conducted by an Association of Friends of Evangelical Truth*, June 1, 1810.

30 Mary to Barnabas, February 26, 1807, Box 1, Folder 12.

31 Dr. Erastus Sergeant, son of missionary Reverend John Sergeant, was the first doctor in Stockbridge and Mary Bidwell's cousin.

32 Deacon of the church during the Deane-Fisk excommunication and one of two guardians of the Deane children.

33 Pamela Sedgwick's condition may not be perfectly understood even now but suffice it to say that while treatment for physical issues was often inept, treatment of mental health issues was contributory to further suffering.

34 Judge Marshall, a Federalist, Chief Justice of the US Supreme Court, was one of two judges who presided over the trial for treason of Aaron Burr. It ended in a verdict of not guilty.

35 Mary to Barnabas, February 17, 1806, Box 1, Folder 9.

36 Barnabas to Mary, February 13, 1806, Box 1, Folder 9.

37 Mary to Barnabas, February 17, 1806, Box 1, Folder 9.

38 Mary to Barnabas, January 26, 1806, Box 1, Folder 9.

39 Edwards was Burr's uncle and the man who raised him after the death of his parents. They were Mary's cousins.

40 Brian Burke, "The Grand Lottery of Life," 2007, p. 1.

41 I am indebted for this wonderful description to Jonah Bader, Yale University, "Candidate for Eternity: The Tumultuous Life of Barnabas Bidwell," unpublished paper, May 2015.

42 "A Sketch of the Life," *Panoplist*, ed. Jeremiah Evarts, Boston, January, 10, 1810, Berkshire Athenaeum, v Stockbridge Misc. 10, x3688.

43 Mrs. Charles A. Bidwell, letter of May 25, 1942: "... I found in the Registry of Deeds office in Pittsfield the Power of Attorney which he [Barnabas Bidwell] gave to his attorneys, whereby he turned over his estate to settle all reasonable claims before he left the country. The Clerk of Courts found that the sum he was accountable for was but $303.64. The Federalist newspapers spread the story that he absconded with $12,000 and that information is still being repeated by historians and biographers. The bookkeeping had been done by several clerks in his absence in Washington and Boston, as he was county treasurer while he was a Congressman."

44 See chapter 7.

45 "The Honorable Mr. Sedgwick's Political Last Will and Testament," Evans Digital Edition, Early American Imprints, # 37645, Horatio Jones & Co., from a Republican press, 1800.

46 A. S. Bidwell (Tyringham) to Josiah Brewer (New Haven), May 19, 1819, transcribed by great-granddaughter Helen Bidwell Lukeman, June 1940, Yale University Manuscripts and Archives, Bidwell Family Correspondence, Box 1.

47 Mary to Barnabas, January 13, 1807, Box 1, Folder 12.

Chapter 6 Women and the Law

1 Henry Harrison Sprague, *Women Under the Law in Massachusetts*. Boston: Little Brown & Co., 1903, p. 68. By 1903 the author notes this law had changed and wives "had peace against their husbands."

2 See chapter 4.

3   The Pittsfield Elm was a large and ancient tree located on the square, considered the heart of the town.

4   Smith, *Pittsfield*, p. 437.

5   See chapter 3.

6   See chapter 4.

7   Mary Beth Norton, Liberty's Daughters. Ithaca, NY: Cornell University Press, 1980, p. 41.

8   *Colonial Laws of Massachusetts,* Boston: Rockwell and Church, 1887, p. 101.

9   Ibid., p. 46.

10 Mary Beth Sievens, *Stray Wives*. New York: New York University Press, 2005, p. 94.

11 Commonly listed as grounds for divorce as well as "has left my bed and board."

12 Nancy Cott, "Divorce and the Changing Status of Women in Eighteenth Century Massachusetts," *William and Mary Quarterly* (www .JSTOR.org) 192.80.65.116, p. 588.

13 Ibid., p. 612.

14 *Memoir of Mrs. Abigail Bailey written by Herself,* ed. Ethan Smith, Boston: Samuel T. Armstrong, 1815.

15 Ibid., pp. 58–59.

16 *Acts and Laws of His Majesty's English Colony.* New London: Timothy Green, Printer to the Governor, 1750, p. 197.

17 William Henry Whitmore, Record Commissioner, *Colonial Laws of Massachusetts.* Boston: City Council, 1672–1686, p. 54.

18 George Washington, *Rules of Civility and Decent Behavior in Company and Conversation.* Reprinted by the Colonial Williamsburg Association, 2011, p. 4.

19 With gratitude to the gentleman and fellow researcher who shared the following letter with me from his collection of family memorabilia.

20 Supreme Judicial Court, Berkshire County, Book 2, September term, pp. 341–342.

21 Mary Beth Norton, *Liberty's Daughters*. Ithaca, NY: Cornell University Press, 1980, p. 138.

22 Laurel Thatcher Ulrich, *Good Wives*. New York: Vintage Books, 1980, p. 102.

23 Ibid.

24 See chapter 3.

Chapter 7 Women and War

1   Statement given to the Stockbridge Town Selectmen, April 6, 1776, signed Samuel Brown, Erastus Sergeant, and Asa Bement, Berkshire Athenaeum, Knurow Collection, Volume 11, p. 703.

2   In other accounts Hannah's last name is spelled Duston, Dunston, and Durstan.

3   Herbert Milton Sylvester, *The Indian Wars of New England*. Boston: W. B. Clarke, 1910, pp. 487–488.

4   Kathryn Whitford, "Hannah Dustin: The Judgment of History." *Essex Institute Historical Collections*. Vol. CVIII, No. 4 (October 1972), 304–325.

5   Cotton Mather, *Magnalia Christi Americana*. London, 1702; Hartford: Silas Andrus & Sons, 1853; 1967, II, 634–636.

6   The dates of the French and Indian War are 1754–1763 in America and 1756–1763 in Europe. In New England it was also called the second French and Indian War to note earlier skirmishes in the colonies.

7   Electa F. Jones, *Stockbridge Past and Present*. Springfield: Samuel Bowles & Co., 1854, p. 82. Also see J. A. E. Smith, *The History of Pittsfield, Massachusetts, From the year 1734 to the year 1800*, Boston: Lee and Shepard, 1869, p. 103.

8   Ibid., p. 87.

9   Ibid.

10 Ibid., pp. 35–36.

11 Approximately $28,000 in buying power.

12 Smith, *Pittsfield*, pp. 184–186.

13 Ibid.

14 Ibid.

15 Ibid.

16 National Women's History Museum, www.nwhm.org/education-resources/biography/lydia-barrington-darrragh.

17 Carol Berkin, *Revolutionary Mothers*. New York: Vintage Books, 2003, p. xi.

18 David Hackett Fischer, *Washington's Crossing*. New York: Oxford University Press, 2006, pp. 199–200.

19 Edwin Satterthwaite Parry, *Betsy Ross: Quaker Rebel*. Philadelphia: John C. Winston Co., 1932.

20 Ibid.

21 Philip Young, *Revolutionary Ladies*. New York: Alfred A. Knopf, 1977, pp. 58–59.

22 Ibid., pp. 25–26.

23 Ibid, p. 46.

24 Sally Smith Booth, *Women of '76*. Winter Park, Fla.: Hasting House Press, 1974, pp. 55–57.

25 Also spelled Sampson.

26 They were in fact sisters-in-law Grace Waring Martin and Rachel Clay Martin.

27 Ray Raphael, *A People's History*. New York: The New Press, 2001, p. 157.

28 Some historians dismiss the Sheffield Resolves; others believe Jefferson had them in hand as he wrote, and they call the Sheffield Resolves the first American Declaration of Independence.

29 Cemetery, Stockbridge, Massachusetts; Freeman is buried next to Catharine Sedgwick, author of the eulogy.

30 Ratified 1789.

31 Christina Marquand and Sarah Sedgwick, *Stockbridge 1739–1939*. Great Barrington, Mass.: Berkshire Currier, p. 161.

32 Ibid., p. 162. The exact words vary with each storyteller, but the meaning is always the same.

33 Miles, "Anna Bingham," p. 294.

Chapter 8 Revolution in Women's Lives and Roles

1 Laws are enacted state by state; the earliest date is chosen, so while married women in Connecticut had limited property rights in 1809, it was 1848, thirty-nine years later, before a property rights law was passed in New York State.

2   Timothy Dwight, *Travels in New England and New York*. New Haven, CT: self-published, 1821, II, p. 87.

3   Nathaniel Hawthorne, "The Duston Family," *The American Magazine of Useful and Entertaining Knowledge* (May 1836), n. 397.

4   Whitford, "Hannah Dustin: The Judgment of History."

5   E. L. Doctorow, *The Waterworks*. New York: Random House, 1994.

6   John Blum, *The National Experience*. New York: Harcourt Brace & World Inc., 1963, p. 212.

7   Rollin H. Cook Collection, Great Barrington, p. 227.

8   James R. Miller, *Early Life in Sheffield: From Settlement to 1860*, Sheffield Historical Society, 2002, p. 97.

9   King Township Police Report posted online www.canada.odmp.ord/officer/696-high-constable-john-fisk.

10 Catharine to Frances Sedgwick Watson, March 28, 1819, Catharine Marie Sedgwick Papers, Massachusetts Historical Society, Box 1, Folder 5.

11 Ibid.

12 Catharine to Robert Sedgwick, March 24, 1819, Box 1, Folder 5.

13 Ibid.

14 *The Letters of William Cullen Bryant*, eds. William Cullen Bryant II & Thomas G. Voss. New York: Fordham University Press, 1977, p. 67.

15 Julius to his wife Lucy Forbes Walker Rockwell, The Judge Julius Rockwell Collection, Lenox Library Special Collections, Rockwell Family Letters Compiled by Samuel Forbes Rockwell, 2 volumes.

Appendix I Importance of the French and Indian War

1   William Williams Collection, Israel Williams to William, Index, p. 189.

2   One of "our own Indians" was killed in Stockbridge causing great difficulty. See Electa F. Jones, *Stockbridge Past and Present*, p. 81.

3   William Williams Collection, William Williams to William Alexander, Index, p. 134.

4   *The Correspondence of William Shirley*, ed. Charles Henry Lincoln, New York: Macmillan Company, Volume 2, pp. 122–125.

5   William Williams Collection, Israel Williams to William Williams, Index, p. 189.
6   William Williams Collection, William Williams, Index.

Appendix II The Revolutionary War and Property Confiscation

1   Mary to Barnabas, February 17, 1806, Box 1, Folder 9.

Appendix III The Revolutionary War and the Constitutionalists

1   Smith, *Pittsfield*, p. 358.

Appendix IV Eighteenth-Century Political Parties

1   Smith, *Pittsfield: Volume 2*, p. 108.
2   Ibid.
3   Ibid., p. 109.

Appendix VI Weakening of the Church

1   Popular eighteenth-century saying—meaning, literally, "cheap to purchase" as well as "easy come, easy go."
2   Lenox Town and Selectmen Meetings, Lenox Town Hall.
3   Rollin H. Cooke Collection, Great Barrington, Vol. 15.
4   Samuel Burnham, *The Reverend Thomas Allen*. Cambridge: Welsh Bigalow & Co. 1869, p. 4. Reprinted in *New England Quarterly*, June 1957, Vol. 30, # 2, pp. 147–165.
5   Ibid.

Name Index